A Taste *of the* Maritimes

LOCAL, SEASONAL RECIPES THE WHOLE YEAR ROUND

ELISABETH BAILEY

NIMBUS
PUBLISHING

Nimbus Publishing Limited
3731 Mackintosh St, Halifax, NS B3K 5A5
(902) 455-4286 nimbus.ca

Printed and bound in China

Author photo: Nancy McCarthy
Interior and cover design: Kate Westphal

Library and Archives Canada Cataloguing in Publication

Bailey, Elisabeth
A taste of the Maritimes : local, seasonal recipes the whole year round /
    Elisabeth Bailey.
ISBN 978-1-55109-869-2
1. Cooking—Maritime Provinces. 2. Cookery,
Canadian—Maritime style. 3. Cookbooks— I. Title.

TX715.6.B32 2011   641.59715   C2011-903909-5

Nimbus Publishing acknowledges the financial support for its publishing
activities from the Government of Canada through the Canada Book Fund (CBF)
and the Canada Council for the Arts, and from the Province of Nova Scotia
through the Department of Communities, Culture and Heritage.

Contents

Acknowledgements

I would like to first thank my husband, John Frauzel, without whose voluminous support and encouragement I would not be writing this today. My love and appreciation also goes to our dear son and my favourite sous-chef, Charlie Frauzel. I owe a special debt of thanks to three women: my photographer, Nancy McCarthy, whose creativity, hard work, and artistic vision were fundamental to bringing this project to completion; Joan Bruneau of Nova Terra Cotta Pottery, who generously offered the use of her exquisite pottery for our photo shoots; and Alice Burdick, who has been a wonderful friend, fellow writer, and champion of my work since the day I first conceived of a book about seasonal food in the Maritimes.

I am extremely obliged to the many friends, family, and food producers who have helped me along my path, especially Naomi King, my father Stephen Bailey, my aunt Sallea Wood, Mimi Fautley, Susan Bone, Susan Stephen, Bruce Wildsmith, Kevin Veinotte, Richard Wetmore, Lynne MacKay, Brian Boates, Joanne Schmidt, Carolyn VanDine, Fred Dollar, Jeanita Rand, Nilanjana Das, Faye Labelle, Svenja Dee, Ellen Agger, Meredith Bell, Heather McCallum, Mike Bienstock, and Shannon Sponagle.

Sincere and appreciative thanks go to Patrick Murphy, Kate Kennedy, and everyone else at Nimbus who offered me the chance to publish and nurtured the process with consummate professionalism. I would also like to thank all the fine folk at the Lunenburg and Mahone Bay farmers' markets—they are too many to name, but too wonderful to omit.

Finally, I offer deep and abiding thanks to my mother, Susan Bailey, the person who taught me passion for good books—and, of course, how to cook.

Introduction

Local, seasonal eating is a great idea for many reasons. Consuming the highest quality, most nutritionally dense food you can find? Check. Promoting sustainable environmental practices in the face of uncertain times? Check. Supporting a locally based economy over international conglomerates? Check. Paying primarily for actual food rather than marketing, long-distance transportation, packaging, and storage? Check.

But when push comes to shove, there's one reason that rises to the top of my list of reasons to eat locally and seasonally, and here it is:

Joy.

Eating healthy local foods makes my body more energetic—and life more enjoyable—every second of every day, not just when I'm at the table. What's more, as I have become familiar with local food I've also developed a rich network of social connections through shopping at my local farmers' market—an entire aspect of our community that I would completely miss out on if I bought all my groceries at the supermarket. I feel connected to the land and the people around me, and it makes me happy.

But most of all, fresh local food simply tastes better than its conventional counterparts. And not just a tad better, either; oceans and fields of pleasure better.

When it comes to increasing the joy of local and seasonal eating, though, we have a ways to go. Over 90 percent of food eaten in the Maritimes today is imported. At the same time, local farmers struggle to make their farms profitable while they produce healthy, fresh, delicious food for their neighbours and communities.

The good news is that the Maritime region is the very picture of a rich and eco-diverse local food system. Between the resources of our farms, forests, and waterways and the rich Maritime traditions of making and eating farm- and sea-fresh foods, our potential to feed ourselves is enormous. We simply have to make wise and full use of the resources already in our grasp.

For most people, this starts with buying more local food. While I strongly encourage people to visit their local farmers' market if and when they can, I recognize that it's not a possibility for everyone. Farm markets, CSAs (community supported agriculture), buying co-ops, and natural food stores are all great sources for local and seasonal foods. In addition, many local foods are available at supermarkets. The more people buy (and ask for), the more this trend will increase. Like any business, supermarkets want to meet their customers' needs—so don't be afraid to make your voice heard.

The following are recipes for everyday eating. They include sauces and stocks to freeze or use during busy times, an assortment of reasonably easy recipes for daily meals, and a few special dishes for the holidays. I warmly encourage you to double or triple recipes and freeze your leftovers—it's a relatively low-effort way to make your own convenience food. You might not have the time to cook every evening, but that doesn't mean that you can't enjoy at least some local food every day.

A few notes on the ingredients: While I specify local ingredients in instances where I consider it particularly important, my hope is that you will source ingredients as locally as possible in all cases, especially meats and produce. Second, several recipes call for a pint of this or that. If you don't buy your produce in pints, simply substitute 2 cups per pint. Finally, "butter" always means salted butter. If you happen to have unsalted butter on hand, however, by all means go ahead and use it. Adjust salt to suit your taste (as you should always free free to do anyhow).

In the end, I hope this book will show you how a little effort can pay off with a lot of pleasure. You don't have to do everything "right"; just get in the kitchen and fool around. Have fun. Experiment. If you have any questions about making substitutions, preserving or freezing food, or just what the heck to do with that monster eggplant you bought on impulse at the farmers' market, let me know! Contact me on my website at ElisabethBailey.com, on the Facebook fan page for *A Taste of the Maritimes*, or on Twitter at ElisabethBailey. I look forward to supporting your exploration—and hearing about the joy that local, seasonal eating brings to your life.

Spring

Welcome, spring! In this season, the length of the days surpasses the length of the nights. As the light increases, the scents of awakening life infuse the air. Streams run, as does the sap in the maple trees. Birds sound off into the cool air, and the earth, although still chilly, kicks off its frost blanket and begins to stir. Farmers' markets open and the first fresh things appear in their booths. Young lambs are slaughtered for Easter, one of the few truly seasonal meats in the Maritimes.

Braving stiff winds, flavour-packed blades of green boldly poke up—heralds of things to come. This is the time to enjoy fresh asparagus, fiddleheads, garlic scapes, leeks, chives, mint, parsley, green onions, tender young herbs, salad greens, and the baby leaves of spinach, kale, and chard. Tart, lively rhubarb grows practically in front of our eyes. Small radishes appear and then, later in the spring, strawberries and the first of the beets.

If you're eager to get started on your local foods journey for the year, consider tapping your own maple trees. It's pretty much just a whole lot of boiling, and the resulting syrup will be a sweet promise of the year to come.

Asparagus Omelette   Serves 4

This simple recipe is an ideal way to enjoy fresh and richly nutritious local eggs. I encourage you to visit your farmers' market and try a carton from everyone who sells eggs to see if you find a favourite—I love the multi-coloured eggs I get from Silverlane Farm here in Lunenburg County.

Ingredients
   1 large bunch asparagus, washed, trimmed, and cut into small pieces
   6 large eggs
   ½ cup cream
   ½ teaspoon salt
   ½ teaspoon ground black pepper
   1 ½ tablespoons butter
   1 ½ cups Pan-Fried Criminis (page 105)
   2 tablespoons grated parmesan (available from Fox Hill Cheese House)

Directions
   Steam asparagus pieces for 4–7 minutes or until just tender, then drain well. In the meantime, combine eggs, cream, salt, and pepper in a mixing bowl and whisk until blended.
   Melt butter in a medium-sized pan over medium-low heat. Add steamed asparagus and pan-fried mushrooms and toss to coat in butter. Pour egg mixture over the vegetables. Sprinkle grated cheese on top of eggs. Cook until eggs are cooked through and serve immediately.

A note on asparagus: Instead of cutting off the tough ends of the asparagus stalks for this recipe, try snapping them—they will naturally break at the point where delicious meets stringy. Save the snapped ends for Vegetable Stock (page 59).

Asparagus Omelette

Strawberry Walnut Salad   Serves 4

This salad showcases the tiny, powerful little berries that pop up in lawns around the Maritimes late in the spring. Supported by their cultivated sisters, they polka-dot this dish with bursts of wild flavour. If you don't wish to pick your own, ask at your local farmers' market.

Ingredients
    1 cup walnuts, finely chopped
    3 tablespoons local honey
    1 tablespoon lemon juice
    1 pint fresh strawberries, washed and sliced
    1 pint wild strawberries, gently washed

Directions
    Preheat the oven to 350°F.
    In a mixing bowl, combine walnuts, honey, and lemon juice. Spread on a baking sheet and bake for twelve minutes or until the nuts are slightly browned and fragrant, stirring once.
    Toss warm walnuts with sliced and wild strawberries in a mixing bowl. Serve immediately or chill in the refrigerator to serve later.

Crème Fraîche   Yield: approximately 1 cup

Crème fraîche adds a touch of elegance and richness to many dishes, and it's surprisingly easy to make. It's a particularly lovely accent for fresh spring berries, as in Strawberries with Whipped Honey Crème Fraîche (page 17).

Ingredients
- 1 cup heavy cream
- 2 tablespoons buttermilk

Directions

Combine cream and buttermilk in a glass jar. Cover and shake to thoroughly combine. Let stand at room temperature for 8–24 hours or until mixture starts to thicken. Stir well and refrigerate until ready to use. Will keep in the refrigerator for up to 4 days. Do not freeze.

Strawberries with Whipped Honey Crème Fraîche   Serves 4

A touch of vanilla helps this recipe stand out on the breakfast table. Did you know that the vanilla bean is actually the sex organ of a tropical orchid? Nothing "vanilla" about that!

Ingredients
- 2 cups Crème Fraîche (page 15)
- ¼ cup local honey
- 1 teaspoon vanilla extract
- 3 cups sliced strawberries (lots of other fruits work well here if you'd like to experiment; try it with grated apple and cinnamon!)

Directions

Beat the crème fraîche to soft peaks, then whip in honey and vanilla for 2 minutes more or until fully incorporated. Gently fold in strawberries just as much as needed to combine thoroughly. Serve with a sprig of mint if you've got it—or a smile if you don't.

Savoury Oatcakes   Yield: about 2 dozen oatcakes

Oatcakes have earned their spot as a Maritime heritage food through the tests of taste and time. This savoury version makes a rich yet subtle base for any number of delightful toppings. I like to grace mine with a smear of Fox Hill quark, crumbled bacon, and Caramelized Onions (page 96).

Ingredients

    2 cups rolled oats (such as Speerville New Found Oatmeal)
    1 cup all purpose flour (such as Speerville Whole White Flour)
    2 teaspoons baking powder
    ½ teaspoon salt
    ½ cup butter or bacon grease
    2 teaspoons maple syrup
    ¼ cup cold water

Directions

Preheat oven to 350°F and butter 2 cookie sheets. In a mixing bowl, combine rolled oats, flour, baking powder, and salt. Add butter or bacon grease, maple syrup, and water. Mash with a fork until thoroughly combined into a firm dough.

On a floured surface, roll dough out to a ¼ inch thickness. Cut oatcakes into your desired shape and size. Transfer to cookie sheets and bake for 20–25 minutes or until lightly browned. Cool on racks. Serve with Scape and Ginger Bisque (page 20), Curried Spinach Soup (page 22), or Soldier Bean Soup (page 80).

Speerville Flour Mill

"Supporting the local economy by helping build strong rural communities" …that's the motto at Speerville Flour Mill. Located in the St. John River Valley of New Brunswick, the mill has been supporting local eating through the milling and sale of whole grain flours and cereals in the Maritimes since 1982.

Nearly all of Speerville's bulk grains are sourced in the Maritimes. The mill purchases both wheat and oats, their two top grains, from farmers across Prince Edward Island, Nova Scotia, and New Brunswick. Their oats are a hull-free varietal, which is easier to digest than traditional oats. More nutritious and flavourful than steel-ground flours from large, commercial mills, Speerville's

stone-ground grains also include Red Fife (a descendant of spelt), rye flour, corn flour, corn meal, kamut, and low-gluten buckwheat, rice, and soy flours. I'm especially fond of Speerville's Whole White Flour, a nutritious, unbleached product that can be used in any recipe that calls for white flour.

Speerville grains are widely available at grocery stores across the Maritimes. The company also sells a variety of beans, pastas, dried fruits, and other kitchen staples that are sourced as locally as possible. For more information on Speerville products, visit their website at speervilleflourmill.ca or call at (866) 277-6371.

The crew at Speerville Flour Mill

Scape and Ginger Bisque   Serves 4

This recipe is a convenient and freezer-friendly way to use scapes—those tall, curly, fruiting stalks of the garlic plant that show up in farmers' markets in spring. With its crisp texture and pleasant, garlicky flavour, a garlic scape tastes like the love child of a garlic clove and a green bean.

Ingredients
> 2 cups garlic scapes, snipped into ½-inch pieces
> 2 cups Chicken Stock (page 102)
> ½ cup fresh ginger, peeled and chopped into rough chunks
> ½ cup Crème Fraîche (page 15)
> Salt and pepper to taste

Directions

Combine scapes, stock, and ginger in a stock pot. Heat on medium to a simmer, then cook until scapes soften and just begin to turn drab green, about 20 minutes. Turn off heat, and remove and discard ginger chunks. Add crème fraîche and purée with an immersion blender or remove to stand blender, purée, and return to a clean pot.

Add salt and pepper to taste. Enjoy immediately, or freeze until so moved by your palate.

Curried Spinach Soup   Serves 4

This is my favourite way to use fresh, young spinach, but this recipe is just as delicious with any fresh young green—try it with Swiss chard or even baby kale. It's a great dish for using the Indian spices that, happily, have become part and parcel of Canadian cuisine in recent decades.

Ingredients

> 2 tablespoons butter
> 1 onion, finely minced
> 1 ½ teaspoons salt
> 6 cloves garlic, pressed or minced
> 2 teaspoons ginger powder
> 2 teaspoons ground coriander
> ½ teaspoon ground turmeric
> ½ teaspoon cayenne powder (optional)
> 2 ½ cups Chicken Stock (page 102) or Vegetable Stock (page 59)
> 1 pound young, tender spinach leaves, washed and dried
> 1 cup plain yogurt (available from Fox Hill Cheese House)

Directions

Heat the butter in a large saucepan on medium. Add minced onions and salt and sauté until the onions are translucent. Add the garlic, ginger, coriander, turmeric, and cayenne and sauté for another two minutes.

Stir in the stock and spinach and bring to a boil. Reduce heat slightly and simmer for 10 minutes or until spinach is thoroughly cooked but still a springy shade of green (if it seems drab and militaristic, you've gone too far). Remove from heat and blend, either with an immersion blender or remove to a stand blender and then return to a clean pan. Simmer the purée another couple of minutes, then add yogurt, adjust seasonings if warranted, and serve.

Hint: For good quality spices at a reasonable price, try an Indian grocery store. Mine come from the incomparable Indian Groceries in Halifax.

Fiddleheads with Bacon   Serves 4

A fiddlehead is the tightly coiled crozier of the ostrich fern that grows along river and stream banks in the Maritimes. It's one of the first (and best) fresh tastes of spring, so make the most of them! To prepare fiddleheads for cooking, rinse lightly under running water and pick off any brown leafy bits by hand. Trim off the browned end of the stem along with any tough material. Make sure to always cook fiddleheads thoroughly—while delightful cooked, they are mildly toxic when raw.

Ingredients
   2 cups fresh fiddleheads, cleaned and trimmed
   2 slices local, pastured bacon
   Pepper to taste

Directions
   Pour an inch of water into the bottom of a saucepan and bring to a boil over medium-high heat. If you have a steamer basket, set it in the pan and put the fiddleheads in the basket; if not, set the fiddleheads directly in the water. Cover, reduce heat to medium, and steam or simmer for 8–10 minutes or until you can easily pierce the fiddleheads with a fork.

   In the meantime, fry bacon over medium heat until done to desired crispness. Remove bacon and drain excess bacon grease. I like to save the grease for making Savoury Oatcakes (page 18). Crumble bacon and set aside. Add steamed fiddleheads to the pan and cook for 2 minutes, stirring. Remove from heat, add crumbled bacon and pepper, and serve.

Rooster Scallops   Serves 4

This is the most popular simple scallop preparation at my house, and a perfect easy-yet-elegant dinner when served alongside Fiddleheads with Bacon (page 23). It was originally named for the jaunty rooster who graces the side of the Sriracha bottle (my favourite store-bought Vietnamese-style hot sauce, available at all major supermarkets). Even after I started making my own garlic chile sauce, however, it seemed to fit the spicy flavour that "pecks" at your tongue.

Ingredients
>   1 pound fresh scallops, rinsed and patted dry
>   2 tablespoons extra-virgin olive oil
>   Salt and pepper to taste
>   1 ½ cups local white wine, such as Jost Eagle Tree Muscat
>   2 tablespoons Garlic Chile Sauce (page 60), Sriracha, or favourite hot sauce

Directions
>   Heat a cast-iron skillet on medium-high heat.
>   While the pan is heating up, toss the scallops with olive oil and salt and pepper to taste. Sear over heat for 5–8 minutes (depending on size), turning once. Cut a scallop in half to test for doneness—the interior should be slightly rare but not raw.
>   Remove scallops from the pan, add wine, then quickly scrape up brown bits from the bottom of the pan. Stir, continuing to scrape, for about 4 minutes, then remove from heat. Add garlic chile sauce and stir to blend. Pour sauce over scallops and serve immediately.

Spring Green Meatloaf (with Roasted Cauliflower, page 107)

Spring Green Meatloaf   Serves 6

This is a family standby for showcasing those first green bits of spring, not to mention an affordable way to both enjoy local meats and use up stale bread. Feel free to adjust the recipe to taste—try adding some finely chopped vegetables or substituting Garlic Chile Sauce (page 60) for part of the ketchup if you'd like a little extra kick.

Ingredients

    1 pound local, grass-fed ground beef
    1 pound local ground pork
    1 cup bread crumbs
    1 large onion, minced
    ⅓ cup finely chopped fresh parsley
    2 tablespoons finely chopped fresh chives
    2 large eggs, beaten
    2 large cloves garlic, finely minced or pressed
    ½ teaspoon black pepper
    1 cup Homemade Ketchup (page 58)

Directions

    Put oven rack in middle position and preheat oven to 325°F. Butter a large loaf pan or small baking dish. Wash your hands extremely well with soap and hot water.

    Place all ingredients in a large mixing bowl and combine thoroughly with your hands. Transfer to the loaf pan or baking dish, shaping into a slightly rounded loaf. Bake for 65 minutes or until no pink remains in the centre. Remove from oven and set aside to rest for 10 minutes, then serve.

Yellow Split Pea Stew with Ham and Chives   Serves 8

This dish straddles the seasons as the first chives sprout up, lending their fresh-as-a-fresh-thing taste to a chilly spring evening's dinner.

Ingredients

    1 pound yellow split peas (available from Speerville), rinsed and picked over
    8 cups Chicken Stock (page 102), or Vegetable Stock (page 59)
    3 tablespoons butter
    3 large onions, finely chopped
    ½ teaspoon salt
    ½ pound diced ham
    2 tablespoons chopped fresh chives
    ½ teaspoon dried summer savory, crumbled
    Salt and pepper to taste

Directions

    Combine peas and stock in a large pot. Bring to a boil, skimming off any froth, then reduce heat and simmer, partially covered, until peas are thoroughly cooked and starting to mash, 2 to 2 ½ hours.

    In the meantime, melt butter in a pan over medium heat. Add chopped onions and salt and sauté, stirring, for 15 minutes. Add sautéed onions, diced ham, chives, and summer savory to cooked peas 2 hours into the cooking process. Adjust salt and pepper to taste. If needed, continue to simmer until peas are thoroughly cooked.

Kevin's Natural Meats

"We live in a rainbelt," says Kevin Veinotte of Kevin's Natural Meats in West Northfield, Nova Scotia. "We average an inch of rainfall a week—it's perfect for growing grass. I have fields of grass producing excellent forage that haven't seen a plough in thirty-five years." As a result, the Maritimes make an ideal area for farming grass-fed beef. Significantly more dense in nutrition than its grain-fed counterpart, grass-fed beef contains high levels of Omega 3 acids—a naturally occurring cancer inhibitor.

Kevin and Susan are the seventh generation of Veinottes to farm their land over the last 160 years. For them, growing organically meant a different way of thinking, shifting focus from fixing problems to preventing them. When the Veinottes switched to organic methods a decade ago, they joined the growing ranks of Maritime farmers and food producers who are committed to producing the most healthful, fresh, nutritious, and delicious meats possible. To learn more about Kevin's meats or to order, visit ellora.ca.

To best prepare local, grass-fed meats, I recommend salting meat well before cooking to tenderize it, and slow cooking over low heat, which will break down connective tissues and give you a tender and luscious steak, roast, meatloaf, or burger.

Kevin Veinotte, selling his organic, grass-fed beef at the Lunenburg Farmers' Market

Rhuberry Compote   Serves 6

The proportions in this recipe are not really all that important. Feel free to add more or less rhubarb relative to strawberries. To be honest, I usually don't measure at all—just stew up as much as I have of each on hand. This compote freezes very well, so go ahead and buy all the strawberries you can and use this recipe to save them for a grey day in February. I promise it will be one of the high points of your winter.

Ingredients
　　3 cups sliced rhubarb stalks
　　¼ cup water
　　3 cups sliced strawberries
　　Sugar to taste (start with ½ cup and adjust upwards from there)
　　½ teaspoon allspice (optional)

Directions
　　Combine rhubarb and water in a saucepan over medium heat. Bring to a simmer, stirring occasionally, until rhubarb is tender but not falling apart, about 10 minutes. Add sliced strawberries, sugar, and allspice if using, stirring slowly, until sugar dissolves. Adjust sugar to taste. Transfer to a serving bowl and chill until cold, about 1 hour.
　　Enjoy this compote on its own, with whipped cream, or over vanilla or strawberry ice cream, angel food cake, pancakes, or waffles.

Early Summer

Days reach their longest in early summer, as the earth, air, and water all warm up. This is the "bright" season in the Maritimes—characterized by sunshine and sweet, sharp berry tastes. Strawberries come fully into their own now, and then are joined by raspberries. The first blueberries also start to appear at the market, and herbs such as summer savory, mint, dill, parsley, and thyme arrive on the scene in profusion.

Beans, peas, and squash all have their first season of harvest in early summer. (These three notable classes of vegetables are double-seasoned, with one set of tastes and nutritional profiles now, and another in the late summer or fall.) Enjoy tender green beans raw or lightly steamed, and steam peas or boil them lightly in stock to preserve their character—nature despises a mushy pea. Baby summer squash are an especially delightful treat of this season—almost too cute to eat, their tender skins allow us to enjoy them whole and whole-heartedly.

To best appreciate local food with minimal kitchen work in early summer, I recommend making the most of cucumber—the fresher the better. Try them sliced with a light sprinkle of a flavoured salt, which you can make yourself by mincing fresh herbs and mixing them into your salt.

Spice Berry Pancakes   Serves 4

These fruity pancakes only taste decadent—try them with a side of pastured bacon and local maple syrup for a lazy weekend treat.

Ingredients

    2 ¼ cups all purpose flour (such as Speerville Whole White Flour)

    ¼ cup sugar

    1 tablespoon baking powder

    ½ teaspoon salt

    1 teaspoon cinnamon

    1 teaspoon ground ginger

    2 cups whole milk

    2 large eggs

    3 tablespoons melted butter, plus additional butter for the pan

    1 pint fresh raspberries

Directions

    Preheat a pan or griddle on medium heat.

    In a mixing bowl, thoroughly whisk flour, sugar, baking powder, salt, cinnamon, and ginger. In a second mixing bowl, beat together milk, eggs, melted butter, and raspberries, crushing the raspberries to a pulp in the process.

    Add dry ingredients to wet ingredients and beat until smooth. Coat the heated pan or griddle with melted butter. Working in batches, pour batter by quarter-cupfuls. Cook until bubbles appear and the edges appear dry. Turn pancakes over and cook another 2–4 minutes. Times vary, so keep checking until you get a feel for it.

    Enjoy with Peach Syrup (page 63), maple syrup, or whipped cream.

Balsamic Honey Fruit Salad   Serves 4

Colourful, simple, and classy, this bombardment of berries will make you the toast of any picnic or potluck.

Ingredients
- 1 tablespoon balsamic vinegar (available from Boates Orchards)
- 2 tablespoons local honey
- 1 pint strawberries, hulled and sliced
- 1 pint blueberries
- 1 pint raspberries

Directions

Combine balsamic vinegar and honey in a mixing bowl and whisk to blend. Add all berries and gently toss to coat. Refrigerate for 1 hour before serving.

Boates Orchards

"Traditionally apple cider vinegar is used for pickling—ours makes a superior pickle," brags Brian Boates, the son in the family team behind Boates Orchards. Nestled in the Annapolis Valley of Nova Scotia, Boates Orchards produces organic and non-organic apple cider vinegars for a panorama of uses. Although the family has owned the farm since 1960, they didn't move into vinegar production until 1995. Today, it is their trademark product. Both their unfiltered, unpasteurized organic vinegar and their non-organic vinegars lend body and a fruity undertone to foods far beyond pickles.

In addition to straight-up cider vinegars, the family now produces a pear vinegar, a blueberry vinegar, and a sweet, full-bodied, balsamic-style apple cider vinegar, recommended for spinach greens, salad dressings, and marinades. The farm also offers a U-pick in the fall, featuring Gravenstein, Macintosh, Cortland, Spartan, and Russet apples, as well as unique heritage varieties such as Bishop Pippin and Kings. If you prefer pears, the U-pick offers organic ones in three standard varieties—Clapp, Bartlett, and Bosc.*

Boates vinegars are available at the farm, at the Halifax Seaport Market, through Speerville Flour Mill, at health food stores throughout the Maritimes, and at select Sobeys stores. For more information, visit their website at home.xcountry.tv/~kb/.

Sesame Herbed Fish Cakes   Serves 4 as a main dish or 8 as an appetizer

I won't lie; there's a lot of mincing in this one, although the results are worth it. If you have a food processor you can first roughly chop the ingredients by hand, then mince them in the food processor.

Ingredients
   1 ½ pounds boneless skinless haddock or cod fillets, finely minced
   1 large onion, minced
   ½ cup minced fresh parsley
   ½ cup minced fresh basil
   2 tablespoons minced oregano
   3 ½ tablespoons sesame oil
   1 ½ teaspoons salt
   1 teaspoon pepper
   2 tablespoons bacon grease, butter, or a mixture of both

Directions
   Combine fish, onion, parsley, basil, oregano, sesame oil, salt, and pepper in a large mixing bowl. Wash your hands very thoroughly with soap and hot water, then use wet hands to completely blend the mixture. Shape fish cakes, using a third of a cup of mixture per cake.
   Heat bacon grease or butter in a large pan over medium heat. Working in batches, sauté cakes until cooked through, about 5 minutes per side. Transfer to plate. Serve warm or cold with horseradish sauce, Garlic Chile Sauce (page 60), or Herbed Mayonnaise (page 40).

Herbed Mayonnaise   Yield: roughly 2 cups

This is one of the easiest and prettiest ways to feature fresh, flavourful herbs in your daily diet. Try this mayonnaise with fries, on fish cakes, or in a devilled egg.

Ingredients
> 2 cups loosely packed fresh basil, oregano, or thyme leaves, or a mixture
> 4 springs fresh parsley
> 1 cup mayonnaise
> 2 tablespoons fresh lemon juice
> Salt and pepper to taste

Directions
> Purée the herbs, parsley, mayonnaise, and lemon juice in a blender. (Alternatively you can hand-mince the herbs and stir with mayonnaise and lemon juice to combine.) Season with salt and pepper, then cover and refrigerate for at least 1 hour before serving. Use for Inside-Out Dragon Burger (page 46), Sesame Herbed Fish Cakes (page 39), or Spicy Cod Brandade (page 135). Keeps for up to 3 days in the refrigerator. Do not freeze.

Raspberry Sauce   Serves 4

This recipe gives me the freedom to get "berried away" at the farmers' market! Many farmers will offer a deal if you buy a flat at a time. I freeze the sauce in glass jars and take one out to have with brunch nearly every Sunday all year long.

Ingredients
  2 pints raspberries
  1 tablespoon lemon juice
  Sugar or local honey to taste (start with ¼ cup and adjust upwards if desired)

Directions
  Combine all ingredients in a mixing bowl and mash with a fork until the sauce is consistently syrupy. Use on pancakes, waffles, ice cream, or as a sauce for other fruit. Sauce will keep for up to 1 week in the refrigerator or up to 1 year in the freezer.

Raspberry Sauce served in a pastry shell

Honey Mint Treacle Yield: roughly 1 ½ cups

When you enjoy a local honey, you partake of thousands of summer flowers that entertained the bees. Mix this treacle with sparkling water for a refreshing summer drink or with hot water to soothe a stuffed-up head. It can also be used as a dressing for fruit salad or a drizzle over berry pancakes to give them an extra-special touch.

Ingredients
   1 cup water
   2 cups fresh mint leaves, lightly packed
   ½ cup local honey

Directions
   Combine all ingredients in a pot over high heat. Bring just to a boil, then remove from heat. Let sit for 20 minutes, then strain to remove leaves. Cover and refrigerate. Syrup will keep for up to 1 month in the refrigerator and 1 year in the freezer.

Green Beans with Summer Savory   Serves 4

Summer savory is a traditional herb of the Maritimes. Often used in the place of sage, it has a bouquet and flavour of its own. Farmer John's Summer Savory from Canning, Nova Scotia, is always a good choice for the dried herb if you can't find any fresh.

Ingredients
- 3 cups fresh green beans, washed and snapped (ends snapped off and beans snapped into roughly 1-inch sections)
- 1 clove garlic, finely chopped
- 1 tablespoon minced fresh or 1 ½ teaspoons dried summer savory
- 1 tablespoon extra-virgin olive oil
- ½ teaspoon apple cider vinegar (available from Boates Orchards)

Directions

Bring a medium-sized pot of salted water to a boil over medium-high heat. Add green beans and boil until cooked through but still firm, about 7 minutes. Drain beans and set aside.

Combine garlic, summer savory, and olive oil in a pan and sauté over medium heat for 4 minutes. Add cooked beans to the pan, stir to combine, then add apple cider vinegar. Stir, remove from heat, and serve immediately.

Wine-Poached Cod with Dill   Serves 4

Use this recipe as an opportunity to experiment with a local wine you've never tried before—half can go into the recipe, and half can go into you (and whoever's lucky enough to be your lab partner).

Ingredients

   2 cups dry white wine (such as L'Acadie Blanc or Seyval Blanc)
   2 cups fish stock, Chicken Stock (page 102), or Vegetable Stock (page 59)
   1 pound skinless boneless cod fillet
   2 tablespoons butter
   2 teaspoons minced fresh dill
   2 teaspoons minced fresh parsley
   ½ teaspoon pepper

Directions

   Combine wine and stock in a large pan and bring to a simmer over medium-low heat. Add cod, making sure that liquid covers the fish. Simmer until cod is just cooked through and flakes apart easily, 5–10 minutes depending on thickness.

   While cod poaches, combine butter, dill, parsley, and pepper in a mixing bowl. Mash thoroughly with a fork to combine. Place a heaping teaspoonful on each serving of poached cod and serve.

Inside-Out Dragon Burger   Serves 4

Is there a more summery pleasure than a juicy, homemade burger? Although the directions specify cooking your burgers in a frying pan, you can also grill these on the barbeque with great success.

Ingredients

    2 pounds local, grass-fed ground beef

    1 ½ teaspoons salt

    1 teaspoon pepper

    1 egg, beaten

    4 ½ tablespoons Dragon's Breath Blue cheese from That Dutchman's Farm, Upper Economy, Nova Scotia, or other soft cheese

    1 tablespoon butter

Directions

Combine ground beef, salt, and pepper in a mixing bowl. Gently blend the mixture, then refrigerate for at least 1 and up to 6 hours. (Giving the salt a little time to work on the meat will help the finished burger stick together.)

Preheat a frying pan on the stove over medium heat. Remove beef mixture from the refrigerator, add egg, and mix to combine. Gently form beef mixture into 8 thin patties. Place 1 generous tablespoon of cheese in the middle of 4 patties, then cover them with 4 remaining patties. Gently mould the edges to seal them together.

Melt butter in heated frying pan then add burgers, cooking in batches if they do not all fit at once. (Do not press down on the burgers with a spatula as this will dry them out.) Cook until burgers reach an internal temperature of 160°F. Serve on a bun with Homemade Ketchup (page 58), Caramelized Onions (page 96), Herbed Mayonnaise (page 40), or any other toppings you like.

Chicken with Balsamic Vinegar Glaze   Serves 4

Serve this entrée with Minted Peas (page 49) and Company Tea Cakes (page 50) for a light yet elegant summery dinner with guests.

Ingredients

    2 tablespoons extra-virgin olive oil, divided

    1 ½ pounds local, free-range chicken meat, diced

    ½ teaspoon salt

    ½ teaspoon pepper

    1 tablespoon maple syrup

    ½ cup balsamic vinegar (available from Boates Orchards)

    ¼ cup chopped fresh parsley

Directions

Heat 1 tablespoon of olive oil in a frying pan over medium-high heat. Toss the other tablespoon of olive oil with the diced chicken, salt, and pepper. Add chicken mixture to the pan and sauté until cooked through, about 10 minutes. Remove chicken.

Add maple syrup and vinegar to the pan and boil until slightly thickened while scraping up browned bits from the bottom of the pan, about 3 minutes. Turn off heat and return chicken to the pan. Stir chicken to coat thoroughly with balsamic glaze. Transfer chicken to a plate, sprinkle chopped parsley over the top, and serve.

Minted Peas   Serves 4

Luxury, meet fresh. If green had a taste, this would be it!

Ingredients
    ½ cup Chicken Stock (page 102) or Vegetable Stock (page 59)
    2 cups fresh shelled green peas
    2 tablespoons heavy cream
    1 tablespoon butter
    1 tablespoon minced fresh mint

Directions
    Bring the stock to a boil in a small pot over medium-high heat. Add the peas and continue to boil until cooked, about 6 minutes. Remove from heat. Add heavy cream and butter and stir until butter is melted. Add minced mint, stir to blend, and serve immediately.

Company Tea Cakes   Yield: 6–9 tea cakes, depending on preferred size

Like many others in the Maritimes, my farmers' market is brimming with a gorgeous and tantalizing variety of locally made jams. Even though I rarely eat jam on toast, whenever I see a flavour I just can't resist I go ahead and pick it up—I know I can always use it in this recipe.

Create your own variation by adding one or two elements to pair with the jam. In the tea cakes pictured, I used a lavender strawberry jam from Nova Scotia's Ma Bell Condiments and added a ½ cup of sliced strawberries to the whipped cream. Another favourite of ours is Ma Bell's ginger pear jam—when using it for tea cakes, I add a ½ cup of minced candied ginger and 2 tablespoons of Ironworks pear eau de vie to the whipped cream…you get the idea!

Ingredients
- ¾ cup white cake flour
- 1 teaspoon baking powder
- ¼ cup whole milk
- 2 tablespoons butter
- ¾ cup sugar
- 4 eggs
- 2 cups heavy cream
- 3 tablespoons local honey
- ½ cup locally made jam, any flavour

Directions

Preheat oven to 350°F. Butter and flour a large baking pan (9 by 12 inches or similar) or line it with parchment paper.

Whisk flour and baking powder together in a mixing bowl and set aside. Combine milk and butter in a saucepan over medium-low heat until butter is completely melted. In the meantime, combine sugar and eggs in a second mixing bowl and beat with an electric beater for 4 minutes or until volume triples. Add flour mixture and hot milk and butter mixture to the sugar/egg mixture, gently folding until just combined.

Transfer batter to the prepared baking pan and bake until a knife inserted in the middle comes out clean, 15–20 minutes. Remove and set aside to cool.

In a fresh mixing bowl, combine heavy cream and honey. Beat with an electric beater for 4–5 minutes or until cream is fully whipped and spreadable.

Remove cooled cake from pan and cut into 2–3 inch squares. (If cake is difficult to remove, try cutting squares in the pan and removing each one separately.) Cut each square in half horizontally to create 2 slices. Spread a heaping teaspoon of jam on the bottom slice of each square, then top with 3–4 tablespoons of whipped cream. Gently place the second slice on top and serve.

Galloping Cows Fine Foods

When Joanne and Ron Schmidt started a roadside fruit and vegetable stand at their farm in the Cape Breton Highlands in 1994, they had no idea their produce would end up taking them to the Oscars!

Finding it difficult to clear a profit growing and selling produce, the Schmidts turned to jamming their leftover strawberries. When they found out how well their jam sold they decided to expand beyond strawberries, growing to eventually include a wide range of fruit butters, sauces, and savoury jellies. Using only perfectly ripe fruits and vegetables harvested at the height of their season, the Schmidts rely on Nova Scotia produce to create convenient condiments that can turn a slice of toast, a bowl of oatmeal, or a plain chicken breast into a symphony of local flavour.

Their pepper spreads are an ideal meatball glaze or accompaniment to a local Gouda or cheddar, while sweet selections such as peach sauce with Grand Marnier or German wine rhubarb jam can be used to make a special treat out of a plain cake or ice cream.

One day, an email arrived at the farm inviting the Schmidts to bring their condiments to the Toronto International Film Festival. They created a brandy cranberry marmalade for the occasion. That event led them to the Golden Globes, and then the 2011 Oscars. Now the elite of Hollywood get to eat as well as we do in the Maritimes. (At least until they run out of jam!)

For more information, visit their website at gallopingcows.com *or call (902) 787-3484.*

Ron and Joanne Schmidt, proprietors of Galloping Cows Fine Foods in Cape Breton

Late Summer

The crest of heat follows the crest of light in late summer, and innumerable fruits and vegetables ripen for harvest. The succulence of stone fruits comes to the fore with peaches, cherries, and plums. The Maritimes turn lousy with blueberries and tomatoes. Chiapas Wild, Tigerella, Scotia, Absinthe, Tommy Toe—the varietals of local heirloom tomatoes are stunning.

Zucchini and other summer squash, broccoli, onions, blackberries, bell peppers, hot peppers, and early carrots are all ripe now as well. Mature beans also come onto the market at this time—they aren't always as easy to find as dried beans, but they are a delight when you do. Use them in any recipe that calls for dried beans—simply skip the soaking step and reduce the cooking time to between 30 and 60 minutes, depending on the varietal (do a test taste after 30 minutes to check).

The irony of late summer is that after a day of putting up produce for winter in a hot kitchen, I usually don't feel like cooking! Luckily, it's also a lovely time of year to eat light. Refreshing ripe fruits such as watermelon, cantaloupe, and cherry tomatoes are at the ready to help you keep your cool on sweltering days.

Late Summer Rum and Fruit Salad   Serves 6

Sweet, lightly spiced rum and fresh fruit—a delightfully refreshing combination when you've had about enough of the summer heat!

Ingredients

- 3 tablespoons local honey
- 3 tablespoons rum (available from Ironworks Distillery)
- 2 large, ripe peaches, pitted and diced
- 1 large or 2 small pears, cored and diced
- 1 pint grapes, seeded and halved
- 1 large Honeycrisp or other crisp local apple, cored and diced

Directions

Combine honey and rum in a mixing bowl and whisk to blend. Add fruit and gently toss to coat. Refrigerate for 1 hour before serving.

Homemade Ketchup   Yield: approximately 2–2 ½ cups

Rich and bursting with tomato flavour, this classic ketchup is one of my most popular local food recipes with the under-twelve set.

Ingredients
- 1 teaspoon ground cinnamon or curry powder
- 2 cups Slow-Roasted Tomatoes (page 64)
- 1 large onion, diced
- 1 garlic clove, peeled and smashed
- 1 ½ teaspoons salt
- ½ cup apple cider vinegar (available from Boates Orchards)
- ¼ cup maple syrup

Directions

Combine all ingredients in a large saucepan. Cook over medium heat, stirring occasionally, until the onions are very soft, about 1 hour.

Turn off the heat, let the mixture cool slightly, then purée with an immersion blender or transfer to a stand blender, then back to a clean pot. Turn the heat back on to medium and cook, stirring occasionally, until the mixture has thickened and darkened slightly in colour, about 30 minutes. (If the mixture starts to scorch, turn down the heat a bit.)

Transfer the ketchup to a glass container, cover, and refrigerate overnight to allow flavours to blend. Ketchup will keep in the refrigerator for up to 3 weeks and in the freezer for up to 1 year.

Vegetable Stock   Yield: approximately 2 quarts

One of the most marvellous things about this recipe is its flexibility—you can really put any vegetable or combination of vegetables in it and end up with something delicious; it also freezes perfectly. Having this recipe in your back pocket gives you the freedom to buy anything that's at the height of its season, irresistibly priced, or simply irresistible, without necessarily knowing how you'll use it. If nothing else inspires, you can always make stock and preserve the vegetables' flavour and nutrition until the day you need it. You can put many odds and ends in vegetable stock—"waste" such as corn cobs, organic onion skins, and green carrot tops make a fine stock and help you get the most bang for your buck.

Ingredients
    ¼ cup extra-virgin olive oil
    1 pound carrots, peeled and cut into large chunks
    2 large onions, peeled and roughly chopped
    2 bell peppers, any colour, seeded and roughly chopped
    4 garlic cloves, peeled
    2 bay leaves
    ¼ cup dried dulse (this traditional sea vegetable is a valuable source of iodine)
    4 sprigs fresh parsley
    5 sprigs fresh thyme or dill
    Salt and pepper to taste

Directions
    Preheat oven to 425°F.
    Combine olive oil, carrots, onion, bell peppers, and garlic (or any other firm, bulky vegetables you are using) in a large baking pan. Roast, stirring occasionally, for 40 minutes.
    Transfer contents of the roasting pan to a stock pot or crock pot. Add bay leaves and dulse and fill with water until vegetables are just covered. Cover and bring to a simmer. Continue to simmer for 1 ½ hours in a stock pot, or 3 hours in a crock pot. Add parsley, thyme, dill, or any other herbs or leafy greens you are using. Simmer for another 20 minutes, then turn off the heat. Remove large solids with a slotted spoon. Pour the stock through a sieve, then add salt and pepper to taste. Keeps for up to 1 week in the refrigerator and 1 year in the freezer.

Garlic Chile Sauce   Yield: approximately 2 cups

Warning: You might want to wear protective gear for this one! Whatever you do, after making this sauce do NOT touch your eyes or mouth until you have thoroughly washed your hands. Wash vigorously with soap and water, then, under running water, rub your hands along something made from stainless steel—this process eradicates the traces of volatile oil that soap can't quite remove.

Ingredients

    1 pint hot peppers (jalapeño, habanero, Scotch bonnet, or any other hot
       pepper available from your local farmers)
    2 large heads garlic
    ¾ cup white vinegar

Directions

Roughly chop peppers and garlic, then combine in a pot with vinegar. Heat over medium heat to a simmer, then cook for 20 minutes.

Purée with an immersion blender or transfer to a stand blender. Seal in a glass jar. Use in the recipes in this book or to add spice to any dish—a teaspoonful at a time! Sauce will keep in the refrigerator for up to 1 month or in the freezer for 1 year.

Peach Syrup

Yield: approximately 2 cups

Some people think that oranges taste like sunshine, but I've always thought that peaches capture the spirit of a sunny, summer day the best of any fruit. Tuck a little of this syrup in the back of your freezer to brighten up a rainy day later in the year.

Ingredients

　　2 pounds very ripe peaches, pitted and chopped
　　½ cup local honey or to taste
　　2 teaspoons lemon juice

Directions

　　Combine all ingredients in a pot and cook over medium heat, stirring occasionally, for 15 minutes. Pour mixture through a strainer, pressing firmly to extract liquid. Discard solids left over. Syrup will keep in the refrigerator for up to 1 week or the freezer for up to 1 year.

Peach Syrup served with yogurt parfait

Slow-Roasted Tomatoes   Yield: approximately 3 cups

These freeze beautifully, so stock up during tomato season and enjoy fresh roasted flavour all winter long. Use them for sauces, stews, soups, pizza, or Basic (ally Fabulous) Tomato Sauce (page 66).

Ingredients
- ¼ cup extra-virgin olive oil
- 4–5 pounds tomatoes (paste tomato varietals are ideal but this recipe works with just about any kind of tomato that appeals to you)
- 1 head garlic, cloves separated and peeled
- 1 teaspoon salt

Directions

Preheat the oven to 250°F. Prepare a baking sheet by brushing it with the olive oil. Slice small and medium-sized tomatoes (including paste tomatoes) in half and larger tomatoes in quarters. Place them cut side down on the sheet.

Add garlic cloves here and there between the tomatoes and sprinkle salt evenly. (If you happen to have some rosemary leaves on hand you can sprinkle those on as well). Slide the sheet into the oven and roast for 5–7 hours, until tomatoes are wrinkled and the flesh separates easily from the skins. If the edges are starting to burn, take them out.

Allow tomatoes to rest for 15 minutes, then remove skins and discard. Use immediately or store in a container until ready to use. Tomatoes will keep in the refrigerator for up to 1 week or the freezer for up to 1 year.

Basic (ally Fabulous) Tomato Sauce   Yield: variable

Although most tomatoes are red, Maritime farmers also grow yellow, orange, pink, purple, green, blue, and black varietals, as well as ones with yellow, orange, pink, or green stripes. Several tomatoes have been developed at the agricultural research station in Kentville, Nova Scotia, including the Scotia, the Kenearly, the Cabot, and the Fundy. Look for these at your local farmers' market for a literal taste of local history.

Ingredients

As many tomatoes as will fit in your largest pot or pan, any varietal or
   combination of varietals

½ teaspoon salt per pound of tomatoes

Directions

Roughly chop tomatoes and combine with salt in the pot.

Warm on medium-low heat and cook until broken down completely, 2–3 hours. You can either pick out the curled-up skins with your fingers (which is what I usually do) or strain the resulting sauce through cheesecloth to get seed-free tomato sauce. I like my sauce rustic with at least some of the seeds in it, so I skip the straining, but if you don't care for seeds, this step is really quite easy.

You can put this plain sauce in freezer containers and freeze for winter, or add other ingredients, and then freeze. One big pot of tomatoes = several delicious winter meals of homemade spaghetti sauce. Whip these out when unexpected company comes—they'll think you're a genius. (And they'll be right. After all, you took my advice, didn't you?)

I almost always add other ingredients before freezing because I usually have other produce fresh from the market lying around that I want to make the most of while it's at the height of its nutritional value. I don't plan what I'll put in my sauce too carefully, I just use whatever I happen to have. Pretty much any combination of the following ingredients will work:

Slow-Roasted Tomatoes (page 64)
Minced Oven-Dried Tomatoes (page 70)
Garlic
Sautéed onion
Caramelized Onions (page 96)
Roasted bell peppers (any colour)
Roasted spicy peppers (if you swing that way; I do)
Herbs (especially basil, thyme, rosemary, and oregano, but also marjoram, parsley, and cilantro)
Pan-Fried Criminis (page 105)
Cooked corn
Roasted eggplant
Crushed green peppercorns

…or, really, anything you like. Sometimes I crumble some cooked bacon or add some browned ground pork or beef (locally produced, of course) and freeze it as a meat sauce.

Coffee Barbeque Sauce Yield: approximately 4 cups

Use this pungent and mildly addictive sauce on the Barbeque Ribs with Sauerkraut (page 81), grilled chicken, or as a glaze for roasting vegetables.

Ingredients

2 tablespoons extra-virgin olive oil

1 ½ cups chopped onions

6 garlic cloves, peeled and minced

1 hot pepper (jalapeño, habanero, Scotch bonnet, or similar), seeded and minced

2 tablespoons chili powder

½ cup maple syrup

2 tablespoons chopped fresh cilantro

1 teaspoon ground cumin

2 large tomatoes, diced

1 cup Chicken Stock (page 102) or Vegetable Stock (page 59)

1 cup freshly brewed strong coffee (Laughing Whale French Roast is ideal, but any strong coffee will do the trick)

Salt and pepper to taste

Directions

Warm the olive oil in a saucepan over medium-high heat. Add onions, garlic, and hot pepper; sauté until onions are tender, about 8 minutes. Add chili powder, maple syrup, cilantro, cumin, diced tomatoes, stock, and coffee. Bring mixture to a boil. Reduce heat to medium-low and simmer uncovered, stirring occasionally, for 40 minutes. Add salt and pepper to taste. Use immediately or chill until ready to use. Sauce will keep in the fridge for up to 1 week or in the freezer for up to 1 year.

Canadian Organic Maple Company

Canadian Organic Maple Company in Divide, New Brunswick, is the largest producer of organic maple syrup in the world. Owners Gus and Sandra Hargrove produce an average of 22,000 gallons of certified organic syrup a year from the Appalachian hardwood forest that surrounds Divide—so named because it sits at the watershed between the St. John River and the Miramichi.

The excellence of the company's product is widely recognized. It won a first place award in the amber category at the 2003 North American Maple Syrup Council conference in Truro, Nova

Scotia. In 2004, the North American Maple Council awarded Canadian Organic the prize for Best Maple Products. In 2005, Canadian Organic Maple Syrup won second place in an international contest between seven hundred sweeteners.

In addition to their excellent maple syrup, the company produces maple spread and other maple products for specialty markets. Use the "contact us" form on their website at canadianorganicmaple.com *for more information.*

Gus and Sandra Hargrove of Canadian Organic Maple Company at their maple woods in Divide, New Brunswick

Oven-Dried Tomatoes   Yield: approximately 2 cups

Dried tomatoes can be enjoyed as they are or rehydrated for use in pizza, lasagne, soups, or sauces. To rehydrate, pour boiling water or chicken stock over them and let them sit for about 5 minutes, or until the skins are soft. Drain them in a strainer, saving the liquid. Add it to dressings, soups, and sauces to amp up their flavour and nutrition. Paste tomatoes and cherry tomatoes are the best choices, as they have a high flesh to juice ratio. If you can get your hands on heirloom varietal Principe Borghese, snap them up!

Ingredients
    4 pounds fresh tomatoes
    2 tablespoons salt

Directions

Preheat oven to 175° F. Cut your tomatoes in half lengthwise, removing any bruised parts. If you have paste tomatoes, don't worry about removing seeds; if you have seedy tomatoes, scoop out the seeds with a finger or a spoon.

Spread out your tomatoes on trays (clay trays are especially great but regular metal cookie sheets will do just fine). Don't let the tomatoes touch one another. Sprinkle them lightly with salt. Place the trays in the oven and bake until the tomatoes are shrivelled and dry but still flexible, usually 6–12 hours depending on the size of your tomatoes. Cool thoroughly before storing.

You can store dried tomatoes in freezer bags or covered in extra-virgin olive oil in jars. With either method, they will keep indefinitely in the refrigerator—you don't even need to freeze them, though you can if you wish. Use them chopped in soups, salads, sauces, or Picante Tomato Dip (page 127).

Creamed Corn with Garlic Chives   Serves 6

The secret to great creamed corn (or great anything corn) is to cook it as soon as possible after it is picked. The sugars in the corn convert quickly to starch, making corn an especially important food to enjoy fresh and local.

Ingredients
- 6 ears fresh corn, shucked
- 1 cup water
- 2 tablespoons butter
- ½ cup Crème Fraîche (page 15)
- 2 teaspoons all-purpose flour
- 1 tablespoon chopped fresh garlic chives
- Salt and pepper to taste

Directions

Cut corn off the cobs with a sharp knife. Combine corn kernels, water, and butter in a saucepan. Simmer over medium heat, uncovered, stirring occasionally, until tender, 5–7 minutes. Drain corn and set aside.

Whisk crème fraîche and flour together in a small pan and bring to a boil over medium heat, whisking constantly. Boil for 1 minute, then remove from heat. Add a third of the cooked corn to the crème fraîche mixture and blend with an immersion blender or in a stand blender. Stir chives, salt, and pepper into the blended sauce, then combine with remainder of cooked corn. Serve immediately.

Roasted Vegetable Pastiche   Serves 8

*This is the main recipe (or rather, method, since I'm extremely liberal with
substitutions) that I use to preserve vegetables for winter. Roasted in stock, these
veggies freeze like a dream for a winter's day. Store them in sealed freezer bags
(suck out excess air out with a straw), then simply reheat at will. You can also purée
these vegetables and add extra stock, milk, and/or cream to make a hearty bisque
any time of year.*

Ingredients
    2 cups chopped mushrooms
    3 medium carrots, peeled and thinly sliced
    1 large onion, peeled and coarsely chopped
    1 large red bell pepper, cut into ½-inch dice
    2 large zucchini, sliced
    4 garlic cloves, peeled and sliced
    3 tablespoons extra-virgin olive oil
    2 teaspoons salt
    2 cups Chicken Stock (page 102) or Vegetable Stock (page 59)

Directions
    Preheat oven to 400°F.
    Combine all ingredients in a mixing bowl and toss to combine. Spread
across a rimmed baking sheet. Roast until all vegetables are tender, stirring
occasionally, about 1 hour. Vegetables will keep in the refrigerator for up to 5
days and in the freezer for up to 1 year.

Summer Squash with Apple Cider Crumbs   Serves 4

The bright note of apple cider vinegar adds a descant above the squash symphony in this recipe.

Ingredients
- ¼ cup butter
- 1 cup stale white bread crumbs
- 1 teaspoon apple cider vinegar (available from Boates Orchards)
- 1 ½ teaspoons minced fresh thyme
- 2 garlic cloves, minced
- 2 large or 3 small zucchini or other summer squash, washed and sliced into rounds

Directions

Melt butter in a frying pan over medium heat, then add bread crumbs, vinegar, thyme, and minced garlic. Cook, stirring, until crumbs are golden, about 5 minutes. Remove bread crumb mixture and add zucchini rounds to the pan. Sauté until cooked through, 5–7 minutes. Remove to a serving plate, top with crumb mixture, and serve.

Broccoli in Cheese Sauce   Serves 4

Ah, cheese sauce—that magic ingredient that makes vegetables attractive to people who "don't like vegetables." While broccoli has the perfect structure to pair with this sauce, feel free to use it to slip practically any veggie into your family's diet.

Ingredients
- 1 bunch broccoli
- 2 tablespoons butter
- 2 tablespoons all-purpose flour
- 1 cup milk
- ½ cup Gouda or cheddar, shredded (I like Fox Hill's peppercorn Gouda for this)
- Salt and pepper to taste

Directions

Wash broccoli and cut florets and tender pieces of stalk into bite-sized pieces.

Pour 1 inch of water into the bottom of a saucepan and bring to a boil over medium-high heat. If you have a steamer basket, set it in the pan and put the broccoli in the basket; if not, set the broccoli directly in the water. Cover, reduce heat to medium, and steam for 5–7 minutes or until you can pierce the broccoli with a fork. Immediately remove from saucepan and set aside on a cool plate.

Melt the butter in a saucepan over medium-low heat. Add the flour and stir continually for 2 minutes until thoroughly blended. Slowly add milk, whisking constantly. Cook until mixture begins to thicken, then slowly add shredded cheese while you continue to whisk. Remove from heat, add salt and pepper to taste, pour sauce over broccoli, and serve.

Fox Hill Cheese House

In 2002, Jeanita and Rick Rand's son Patrick told them that he wanted to continue their family farm into its sixth generation in Port Williams, Nova Scotia. The family sat down together and looked at business plans that would guarantee their shared success—and, with the help of retired cheesemaker friend Martin Winkelman, Fox Hill Cheese House was born.

"We are proud that we plant the seed, grow the grass, milk our herd of Holstein and Jersey cows, and use our own milk in all our products," says Jeanita, the official spokeswoman for the farm. The high-quality feed and care of their herd allows the cheese house to offer milk, yogurt, cheese, and gelato made from drug- and hormone-free milk.

The quality of their products hasn't gone unnoticed: Fox Hill has twice won the Florence Cox award from Farmers Dairy for consistently high-quality milk, as well as the 2009 Taste Nova Scotia Quality Driven Member award. Their award-worthy cheeses include cheddar,

feta, parmesran (not a typo—it's their unique version of parmesan!), Gouda, Havarti, and quark.

What's quark, you ask? Not to be confused with the subatomic particle, it's actually a soft, spreadable cheese that can be used as a substitute for ricotta, cottage cheese, or cream cheese.

Many Fox Hill cheeses pair beautifully with local wines and fruits, and not by accident—the Rands work with local wineries to create customized marriages of taste. (Recent pairings include L'Acadie Blanc with medium cheddar and Pomme D'Or with fenugreek Havarti, for instance.)

You can find the Rands at their Port Williams Cheese House and several farmers' markets around Nova Scotia, including their permanent shop at the Halifax Seaport Farmers' Market. For more information about Fox Hill Cheese House products and where to purchase them, visit their website at foxhillcheesehouse.com or call (902) 542-3599.

Rainbow Fried Rice   Serves 4

Use leftover rice and chicken to make this colourful dish for the next day's dinner. If you want to go the extra step to make a true rainbow, include 1 small eggplant, diced, with the peppers and top the finished dish with a seeded and chopped OSU Blue tomato. (Can't find them in your market? Try growing your own—the seeds are available from Annapolis Seeds.)

Ingredients
- 1 tablespoon extra-virgin olive oil
- 1 small carrot, thinly sliced
- 1 medium red bell pepper, cored, seeded, and diced
- 1 medium yellow bell pepper, cored, seeded, and diced
- 1 small hot pepper, minced (optional)
- 1 cup fresh peas
- 1 egg, beaten
- 1 cup chopped cooked chicken
- 2 cups cooked rice
- 1 tablespoon soy sauce
- Pepper to taste

Directions

Heat oil in a sauté pan over medium-high heat. Cook carrot, stirring occasionally, for 2 minutes. Add bell peppers and hot pepper and cook, stirring, for another 2 minutes.

Add peas, sprinkle with pepper, and cook while stirring for another minute.

Remove vegetables and return pan to heat; add egg, chicken, and rice. Cook, stirring constantly, for 3 minutes.

Return vegetables and add soy sauce and pepper. Cook 1 minute more. Take off heat and serve immediately.

Soldier Bean Soup   Serves 4

Serve this soup with Savoury Oatcakes (page 18) and some sliced local cheese for a panoply of Maritime flavour.

Ingredients

1 ½ cups dried soldier beans, available from VanDine Beans

2 tablespoons extra-virgin olive oil

1 large onion, minced

2 garlic cloves, chopped

1 bell pepper, cored, seeded, and diced

1 hot pepper (such as jalapeño, habanero, or Scotch bonnet) cored, seeded, and diced

1 tablespoon ground cumin

3 cups Chicken Stock (page 102) or Vegetable Stock (page 59)

⅓ cup chopped fresh cilantro

Salt and pepper to taste

Directions

Cover soldier beans in water for 1 hour, then drain and rinse. Cover with fresh water in a pot and bring to a boil over medium heat. Cover and reduce heat to medium-low and cook, stirring occasionally, for 1 ½ to 2 hours or until beans are soft but not mushy. Drain cooked beans and set aside.

Heat olive oil in a stock pot over medium-high heat. Add onion, garlic, bell pepper, hot pepper, and cumin. Sauté until onion is tender, about 5 minutes. Add cooked soldier beans and stock.

Bring soup to boil. Reduce heat to medium-low, then cover and simmer for 20 minutes. Remove soup from heat. Transfer 3 cups of the soup to a stand blender, purée, and return to the pot. Stir in cilantro, salt, and pepper to taste. Serve immediately.

Barbeque Ribs with Sauerkraut   Serves 4

Local sauerkraut is a centuries-old tradition in Lunenburg County, where I live. Happily, locally made and delicious sauerkraut is available throughout the Maritimes.

Ingredients

    1 pound sauerkraut
    2 pounds pork spare ribs
    3 cups Coffee Barbeque Sauce (page 68) or store-bought barbeque sauce

Directions

    Preheat the oven to 300°F.
    Use half the sauerkraut to make a bed in the bottom of a baking pan. Lay out the ribs in a single layer on the sauerkraut. Mound the rest of the sauerkraut around the ribs. Spoon the barbeque sauce over the ribs.
    Cover the pan with aluminum foil. Bake for 3 hours.

Peach Blackberry Sin   Serves 4

To peel peaches easily, gently place them in a pot of boiling water for 45 seconds, then remove and plunge them into a bowl of cold water (to keep the heat from cooking them). The skins should shuck right off.

Ingredients
- 1 ½ pounds peaches, peeled, halved, pitted, and sliced
- 1 tablespoon fresh lemon juice
- ¼ cup local honey
- 1 teaspoon ground cardamom
- 1 pint fresh blackberries

Directions
Combine peaches, lemon juice, honey, and cardamom in a mixing bowl, stir to blend, and allow to rest for 10 minutes. Add blackberries and lightly toss. Serve immediately by itself, with whipped cream, or on pancakes.

Peppery Shrimp Chowder   Serves 8

This recipe showcases the stunning diversity of vegetables and seafood available to us here in the Maritimes—serve it to visiting family members you'd like to pressure to move closer.

Ingredients

>   1 medium onion, chopped
>   3 cups diced mixed peppers
>   2 large garlic cloves, peeled and minced
>   2 strips of thick bacon, cooked and crumbled
>   1 bay leaf
>   1 tablespoon butter
>   8 cups Vegetable Stock (page 59)
>   1 cup Slow-Roasted Tomatoes (page 64)
>   1 teaspoon dried thyme
>   2 pounds medium shrimp, shelled and deveined
>   1 pound scallops
>   1 pound crab meat
>   2 tablespoons Garlic Chile Sauce (page 60)

Directions

Combine onion, peppers, garlic, bacon pieces, bay leaf, and butter in a large stock pot over medium heat and cook, stirring often, until softened, about 12 minutes. Add stock and bring to a boil. Reduce heat and simmer, uncovered, for 30 minutes.

Add remaining ingredients and continue to simmer for another 10 minutes or until seafood is just cooked through. Remove from heat and let stand, covered, for an additional 15 minutes, then serve.

Double Blueberry Cobbler   Serves 6

Every varietal of blueberry has its own unique character and flavour—using two together gives a depth to the "blueberriness" of this cobbler that you won't soon forget.

Ingredients

    1 ½ pints large (highbush) blueberries
    1 ½ pints wild (lowbush) blueberries
    2 tablespoons blueberry liqueur, optional (available from Ironworks Distillery)
    ½ cup sugar plus 2 tablespoons
    2 tablespoons cornstarch
    Zest of 1 lime
    Juice from ½ lime
    1 ⅓ cups all purpose flour (such as Speerville Whole White Flour)
    3 tablespoons sugar
    ¾ teaspoon baking powder
    ¼ teaspoon baking soda
    ½ teaspoon ground cardamom
    5 tablespoons cold salted butter, cut into small pieces
    ¾ cup Crème Fraîche (page 15) or heavy cream

Directions

Preheat oven to 375°F with a rack set in the lowest third of the oven.

In a mixing bowl, combine both kinds of blueberries, liqueur (if using), ½ cup sugar, cornstarch, lime zest, and lime juice. Spread the mixture in the bottom of a medium-sized baking pan (9 by 12 inches or similar; there's a little wiggle room here).

In a second mixing bowl, whisk together flour, sugar, baking powder, baking soda, and cardamom. Add pieces of cold butter and crème fraîche or cream.

Wash your hands thoroughly, then run cold water over one of your hands as long as is reasonably comfortable (don't torture yourself). Using your cold hand, quickly knead the dough until just combined, then press down evenly over berry mixture. Sprinkle remaining 2 tablespoons of sugar over the top.

Bake for 45–60 minutes, until crust is crisp, browned, and baked through. Serve warm or cool with whipped cream, whipped Crème Fraîche (page 15), or ice cream.

Fall

As we enter fall the nights cool down, then the days follow suit. This season is full of large, sweet squash made just a bit sweeter by the first tendrils of real cold. These include pumpkin, acorn squash, the enormous blue Hubbards squash, spaghetti squash, butternut squash, buttercup squash, and my personal favourite, Red Kuri. (Also known as Potimarron in French, the Red Kuri is often said to taste like a cross between pumpkin and chestnuts.)

Potatoes, cranberries, carrots, sweet potatoes, onions, and pears all enter their peak now. Some spring vegetables come back in the fall, with subtly different tastes and textures—these include leeks, rhubarb, and many salad greens.

Fall is also the time for apples, one of the oldest, most popular, and most diverse types of produce cultivated in the Maritimes. With varietals as different as Bishop's Pippin, Honeycrisp, Novamac, and Spartan, it's difficult to eat too many. In my opinion if there's ever a time to overindulge, it's not the holidays but at the height of Honeycrisp season!

Autumn Fruit Sauce   Serves 6

This recipe (or rather, method, since there are so many tantalizing variations) is a convenient way to make the most of a bountiful fall harvest.

Ingredients

4–5 pounds of any combination of apples or pears (When we can get them, we
   like 3 pounds Flemish Beauty pears to 1 pound Orange Cox Pippin apples.)
2 tablespoons lemon juice
Sugar to taste (This depends widely on the varietals of apples or pears; I often
   find that ripe pears don't need any added sugar at all.)

Stovetop Directions

Peel, core, and slice your fruit. Add 1 or 2 tablespoons of lemon juice if you're peeling and coring at a leisurely pace, and give it a toss from time to time to keep the apples from browning. If you're zippy or using Cortland apples (which do not brown) you can skip the lemon juice. Cook covered, on medium-low, stirring occasionally, until all the apples break down completely into sauce, from 45 minutes to 2 hours depending on the type of apple. Sugar to taste a few minutes before removing from heat. Fruit sauce will keep for up to 1 week in the refrigerator or 1 year in the freezer.

Crockpot Directions

Place all ingredients in the crock pot and stir to combine. Cover and cook on low for 8–10 hours or on high for 3–4 hours.

Variations

For anise ginger fruit sauce, put 1–3 stars of anise in the pot while the fruit is cooking down. Mince up to 1 cup of candied ginger. Remove anise stars, and add minced candied ginger and white sugar to taste. Purée with an immersion blender, or remove to a stand blender.

For cinnamon fruit sauce, simply add ground cinnamon to taste. Start with 2 teaspoons and adjust upward as desired.

For a more grown-up applesauce that's great on brunch pancakes or as a simple, elegant dessert, add up to 1 cup of red wine for every 2 pounds of apples. Try red wine applesauce with the Marechal Foch from Jost Winery on the

Malagash Peninsula of the Northumberland Strait. For a lighter, fruitier touch, use a Jost fruit wine such as their apple and blueberry Blush or their blueberry, apple, cinnamon, and clove Glowine.

Add mint, rose hips, rosemary, or thyme (great for dressing pork roast if you omit the sugar), a handful of berries, lemon zest, or orange pieces. Use your imagination!

This fruit sauce freezes beautifully. Make lots.

Roasted Butternut and Apple Salad   Serves 8

This classic combination never fails to please.

Ingredients

Dressing
>   4 tablespoons apple-based balsamic vinegar (available from Boates Orchards)
>   4 tablespoons extra-virgin olive oil
>   Salt and pepper to taste

Salad
>   ¼ cup extra-virgin olive oil
>   2 teaspoons local honey
>   1 teaspoon salt
>   1 teaspoon pepper
>   4 pounds of butternut squash, peeled, seeded, and diced
>   3 Cortland apples, cored and diced (substitute Macintosh or Honeycrisp if you don't have Cortland)
>   ½ cup sliced almonds
>   2 tablespoons minced fresh parsley

Directions

Preheat oven to 400°F.

Whisk vinegar and oil for dressing together in a small mixing bowl. Season to taste with salt and pepper. Set dressing aside.

Combine olive oil, honey, salt, and pepper in a second mixing bowl and whisk to combine. Add diced squash and toss. Distribute squash evenly over the baking sheets. Bake for 30 minutes, turning chunks over halfway through.

Allow squash to cool on baking sheets for 10 minutes, then combine with diced apple, almonds, parsley, and dressing in a mixing bowl. Toss to coat. Serve immediately.

Lunenburg Salad   Serves 8

(adapted from The Apple Connection *by Beatrice Ross Buszek)*

The red, purple, and green colours in this easy salad make it particularly attractive for a potluck or company dinner.

Ingredients

    3 Macintosh apples, thinly diced
    1 purple cabbage, thinly sliced
    ¼ cup apple cider vinegar
    1 tablespoon dried mustard
    3 tablespoons peanut oil
    ½ cup shredded fresh basil (optional)
    Salt and pepper to taste

Directions

    Toss all ingredients until just combined. Chill in the refrigerator for at least 1 hour, then serve.

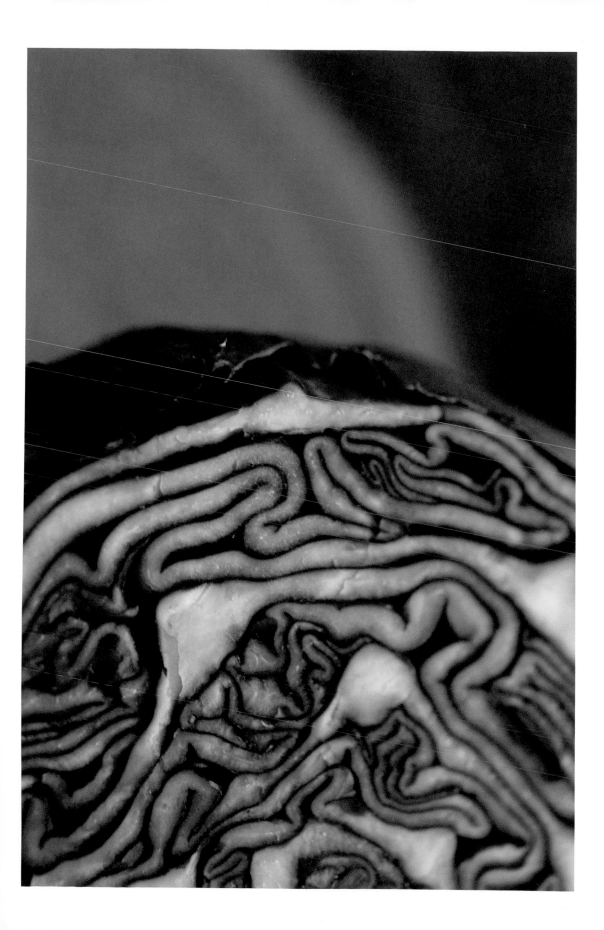

Apple Peel Syrup   Yield: approximately 2 ½ cups

This is a great way to use up apple (and/or pear) peels you remove for pies or picky children. I recommend only making this syrup with organic fruit, as sprayed apples carry a high concentration of pesticides in their otherwise delicious and nutritious peels. Use the syrup for ice cream, pastries, preserving frozen fruit, flavouring drinks, or anything else you like.

Ingredients
    2 cups water or white wine
    1 ½ cups local honey
    Peelings from 4 large or 6 small apples

Directions
    Combine all ingredients in a saucepan over high heat. Stir frequently until syrup takes on the colour of the peels and begins to thicken, about 15 minutes. Remove from heat, strain, and use or store. Syrup keeps in the refrigerator for up to 1 week and the freezer for up to 1 year.

Apple Peel Syrup in sparkling water

Caramelized Onions   Yield: approximately 1 ½ cups

Properly caramelized onions have a sweet, savoury taste that is not identifiably "oniony." I like to freeze portions of about 3 tablespoons each of minced, caramelized onions to toss into soups, stews, and sauces. This adds concentrated flavour that people love (but usually can't identify).

Ingredients
    2 tablespoons extra-virgin olive oil
    2 tablespoons butter
    5 large or 7 medium onions, thinly sliced
    2 teaspoons salt

Directions
    Combine olive oil and butter in the bottom of a large pan over medium-low heat. Add sliced onions and salt; stir to combine. Cook, stirring occasionally, until onions turn completely soft and mahogany brown, 40 minutes to 1 hour. If onions are sticking to the bottom of the pan, add another tablespoon of olive oil and lower the temperature slightly.

    When onions are evenly browned, remove from pan, scraping up all browned bits from the bottom, and serve or store. Caramelized onions will keep in the refrigerator for up to 1 week or in the freezer for up to 1 year.

    Alternative cooking method:

    Place all ingredients in a crock pot, cover, and cook on low for 8–10 hours.

Caramelized Onions served on baguette slices spread with quark

Ciao Ciao   Serves 4

A common problem in the Maritimes is a cruel, chilly end to the tomato growing season—usually before the plants have stopped producing. Many gardeners and farmers are stuck with a big pile of green tomatoes sometime in October. Luckily, there's an easy (and delicious) solution in this not-so-traditional, Italian-inspired chow chow.

Ingredients
- 4 cups finely sliced green tomatoes
- 1 cup sliced onions
- 2 tablespoons salt
- ¾ cup balsamic vinegar (available from Boates Orchards)
- 1 ½ cups sugar
- 1 ½ teaspoons dried oregano
- 1 ½ teaspoons dried basil

Directions

Toss tomato slices, onion slices, and salt thoroughly to combine. Let sit overnight. In the morning, drain, rinse to remove excess salt, then combine mixture in a stock pot with vinegar and sugar. Cook over medium heat, stirring often, until mixture thickens slightly, about a ½ hour. Add oregano and basil and stir to combine. Remove from heat, allow to cool, and serve or store. Ciao Ciao keeps in the refrigerator for up to 2 weeks or in the freezer for up to 1 year.

Note: Like the idea of chow chow, but not the work of making it? Visit your local farmers' market—I just about guarantee you'll find jars of chow chow in abundance.

Remembrance Potatoes   Serves 8

Given the plethora of potatoes that grace our provinces, I had to include this traditional family dish. As Shakespeare said, "rosemary for remembrance." We eat these as part of an annual dinner to remember those we have loved and lost.

Ingredients
    1 cup salt
    3 pounds new potatoes, gently scrubbed clean
    2 teaspoons minced fresh rosemary
    Butter and pepper to taste

Directions
    Heat a stock pot with 2 quarts of water over medium-high heat. Add salt and stir to dissolve.

    Once water begins to boil, add potatoes, cover, and reduce heat to medium. Simmer for 20–25 minutes or until potatoes split easily when stuck with a fork. Drain immediately, but do not rinse.

    Toss the potatoes with rosemary, butter, pepper, and love.

Kentdale Farms

"We grow over a million pounds of potatoes on 70 acres…" says Fred Dollar of Kentdale Farms in Winsloe, Prince Edward Island, "…which is small potatoes compared to a conventional grower!" Luckily, the "small potatoes" he and his wife and son, Vaunda and Kent, grow are mighty enough to stock Sobeys stores across the Maritimes, giving everyday shoppers access to a high-quality, organic, local staple.

Having grown up farming on PEI and watching the food markets change over the years, the Dollars chose to meet local needs by specializing in certified organic potatoes about a decade ago. They produce Gold Rush, a russet-style potato (the best choice for mashing); Satina, a yellow potato similar to Yukon Gold; and Red Norland, a red-skinned potato. To balance their soil, they grow organic wheat in the years both before and after a year of potatoes. The wheat is then sold to Speerville Flour Mill (page 19).

For more information about Kentdale Farm potatoes and where to purchase them, email: kentdale@pei.sympatico.ca.

Potatoes from Kentdale Farms

Chicken Stock   Yield: approximately 2 quarts

The vegetables in this recipe are a classic combination, but keep in mind that you can—and should—make stock with any vegetables you have on hand. In spring, use spring vegetables, in summer, use summer vegetables, and so on. Use your imagination here; when someone in my house has the snuffles I make an Immune System Special by doubling the garlic and adding some slices of ginger and dried chiles.

It's particularly important to use local, free-range chicken for chicken stock. I found out the hard way that stock made from conventional supermarket chicken won't form the nutritionally valuable gelatin that results from free-range chicken (and the taste certainly doesn't compare, either). It's also worth knowing that the purpose of adding vinegar or lemon juice is to create an acidic environment, which allows calcium and other minerals to leach out of the chicken bones and into the surrounding liquid, making a more nutritious stock.

Ingredients

　　Chicken carcass (a roasted chicken stripped of most, but not all, of its meat)
　　1 head garlic, cloves separated and peeled
　　2 large or 3 medium onions, roughly chopped
　　3 stalks celery
　　3 large or 5 small carrots
　　⅓ cup apple cider vinegar or lemon juice
　　2 teaspoons salt

Directions

　　Preheat oven to 420°F. Arrange chicken carcass, garlic, and vegetables in a baking pan, then roast for 30 minutes.

　　Transfer contents of the baking pan to a crock pot or stock pot. Add cider vinegar or lemon juice and salt. Add water until contents are just covered. If using a crock pot, cover, set to high, and allow to simmer for 8–12 hours. If using a stock pot, cover and simmer over medium to medium-high heat for 4–6 hours.

　　At the end of the simmering time, using a slotted spoon remove the bones and big chunks from the stock, then strain the broth through cheesecloth set in a strainer. Chill the resulting stock in the refrigerator for a few hours and strain off the fat that rises to the top. Stock can be used for soup, stews, cooking rice, or as the liquid in any other savoury dish. Stock will keep in the refrigerator for 3 days or in the freezer for up to 1 year.

Chicken Mushroom Soup   Serves 4

This nourishing soup hits the spot on a crisp autumn day. Serve with Spiced Honey Pear Salad (page 106) for a complete meal.

Ingredients
    2 tablespoons extra-virgin olive oil
    ⅓ cup minced green onion
    1 tablespoon minced fresh thyme
    6 cups Chicken Stock (page 102)
    1 pound potatoes, peeled and diced
    2 cups shredded chicken
    1 cup Pan-Fried Criminis (page 105)
    Salt and pepper to taste

Directions
    Heat olive oil in a saucepan over medium-high heat. Add green onion and thyme and sauté for 5 minutes. Add stock and potatoes, then simmer until potatoes are very tender, about 30 minutes.
    Add shredded chicken and mushrooms. Bring soup back to a simmer, then remove from heat. Season with salt and pepper. Serve immediately.

Pan-Fried Criminis   Serves 4

While I like criminis best for this simple preparation, feel free to use any kind of mushroom you have. As Julia Child advised, be sure not to crowd mushrooms in the pan—if yours is too small, sauté in two batches (or two pans).

Ingredients
   4 tablespoons extra-virgin olive oil
   1 pound crimini mushrooms chopped into bite-sized pieces
   Salt and pepper to taste
   4 tablespoons white wine, Chicken Stock (page 102), or Vegetable Stock
      (page 59)

Directions
   Heat oil on medium-high in a cast iron pan or other frying pan for 2 minutes, then add chopped mushrooms. Add salt and pepper and sauté, stirring frequently, until mushrooms brown and shrink noticeably, 5–8 minutes. Turn off heat, add wine or stock to the mushrooms in the hot pan, and scrape up browned bits from bottom of the pan to become part of the sauce. Serve immediately or use in Asparagus Omelette (page 12), Slow-Roasted Tomatoes (page 64), or Chicken Mushroom Soup (page 103).

Spiced Honey Pear Salad   Serves 4

Sweet, spicy, tender, and crunchy all at once, this salad will demand your attention with each bite.

Ingredients

Salad

½ cup chopped pecans
2 tablespoons pine nuts
1 tablespoon local honey
2 small ripe pears, cored and diced (use two different varietals of pears for diversity and added flavour)
3 cups mixed salad greens
2 tablespoons minced tarragon

Dressing

¼ cup extra-virgin olive oil
2 tablespoons balsamic vinegar (available from Boates Orchards)
1 tablespoon local honey
½ teaspoon Garlic Chile Sauce (page 60)

Directions

Preheat oven to 350°F. Combine pecans, pine nuts, and honey in a baking dish and stir to coat. Bake for 12 minutes, then set aside to cool for 10 minutes.

Combine nuts, diced pears, greens, and tarragon in a salad bowl.

Combine all dressing ingredients in a small mixing bowl and whisk vigorously. Drizzle dressing over salad and serve immediately.

Roasted Cauliflower   Serves 4

The great thing about cauliflower, in my opinion, is that it is nearly impossible to overcook. Unlike its fussy cousin, broccoli, cauliflower just keeps soaking up the flavour of whatever you're cooking it in, even as it eventually dissolves into a thick sauce. Use it as a textural sponge for any stock or sauce you like.

Ingredients
   1 head cauliflower, washed and chopped into florets and tender stem slices,
      tough stem discarded
   2 tablespoons extra-virgin olive oil
   ¼ teaspoon salt
   1 cup Vegetable Stock (page 59) or Chicken Stock (page 102)

Directions
   Put oven rack in middle position and preheat oven to 450°F.
   In a mixing bowl, toss cauliflower with olive oil and salt. Transfer to a large baking pan and place in the oven. After 10 minutes, add stock to the pan. Roast, stirring occasionally, for 45 minutes. Serve as a side dish or use for Cauliflower Rosemary Potage (page 108).

Cauliflower Rosemary Potage   Serves 4–6

Good stock is key for this classic soup recipe. To freeze, simply stop before adding cream and pepper, then complete the recipe whenever you come back to it.

Ingredients
    2 tablespoons extra-virgin olive oil
    1 large onion, minced
    ½ teaspoon salt
    1 ½ teaspoons minced rosemary, fresh or dried
    1 batch Roasted Cauliflower (page 107)
    4 cups Chicken Stock (page 102) or Vegetable Stock (page 59)
    1 cup heavy cream
    Pepper to taste

Directions
    Combine olive oil, onion, salt, and rosemary in the stock pot. Sauté over medium heat, stirring frequently, for 15 minutes. Add roasted cauliflower and stock, and heat until soup comes to a simmer. Remove from heat and blend with an immersion blender (or remove to a stand blender, then return to a clean pot). Add cream and pepper. Heat on medium-low for 5 minutes, then serve.

Baked Squash with Walnut Oil   Serves 8

This is a versatile dish—omit the salt and pepper and add ¼ cup maple syrup and ½ teaspoon nutmeg for a sweet squash.

Ingredients
> 2 ½ to 3 pounds winter squash (I like Red Kuri) seeded, peeled, and cut into
> 1-inch pieces
> 1 ½ teaspoons salt
> ½ teaspoon pepper
> ¼ cup butter, melted
> 2 tablespoons walnut oil

Directions
> Position a rack in the middle of the oven and preheat to 400°F.

Toss all ingredients in a mixing bowl. Transfer to a large baking dish and bake until squash is tender and starts to brown, stirring occasionally, about 1 hour. Let stand for 5 minutes and serve.

Haddock Wraps   Serves 4

The Mexican-style spices in this contemporary dish enliven the haddock and cabbage that have nourished generations of Maritimers.

Ingredients
- 1 pound haddock fillets, steamed or poached
- ½ small onion, minced
- ½ cup thinly sliced green cabbage
- 1 tomato, chopped
- 2 teaspoons extra-virgin olive oil
- 2 teaspoons apple cider vinegar (available from Boates Orchards)
- ½ teaspoon cumin
- 1 teaspoon fresh minced oregano
- 1 teaspoon Garlic Chile Sauce (page 60) or other hot sauce
- 4 flour tortillas

Directions

Place cooked haddock in a large mixing bowl and flake with a fork. Add minced onion, cabbage, tomato, olive oil, apple cider vinegar, cumin, oregano, and garlic chile sauce, and toss to combine. Spoon mixture onto tortillas and serve immediately. Top with sour cream, shredded cheese, and salsa if desired.

Heritage Bean Chili   Serves 6

It's our family tradition to fill up on this chili before heading out to trick-or-treat on Halloween—the complex carbohydrates in the beans help to hold off the candy crazies. If you prefer a meaty chili, just add a pound of browned ground beef or diced meat to this recipe with the cooked beans.

Ingredients

    1 cup dried Jacob's Cattle beans (available from VanDine Beans)

    1 cup dried yellow eye beans (available from VanDine Beans)

    3 cups Chicken Stock (page 102) or Vegetable Stock (page 59)

    2 tablespoons extra-virgin olive oil

    1 onion, minced

    2 bell peppers, seeded and chopped

    3 hot peppers, seeded and minced

    3 cups Slow-Roasted Tomatoes (page 64)

    1 12-ounce bottle beer (I like Garrison's Fog Burner for this recipe)

    2 tablespoons apple cider vinegar (available from Boates Orchards)

    2 tablespoons maple syrup

    5 garlic cloves, minced or pressed

    2 tablespoons chili powder

    1 ½ teaspoons ground cumin

    1 ½ teaspoons ground coriander

    Salt and pepper to taste

Directions

Combine Jacob's Cattle beans and yellow eye beans in a large pot and cover them with water until water level is twice as high as the bean level in the pot. Leave to soak for 1 hour.

After the hour is up, drain beans, then just cover with fresh water. Add stock to water and bring beans to a simmer on medium-low heat. Cook, covered, until beans are mostly soft, 1 to 1 ½ hours.

Heat olive oil in a large pot over medium-high heat. Add onion, bell pepper, and hot peppers. Sauté for 10 minutes, then add cooked beans with liquid, roasted tomatoes, beer, apple cider vinegar, maple syrup, garlic, chili powder, cumin, and coriander. Bring to a simmer on medium heat and cook, uncovered, for 45 minutes. Add salt and pepper to taste. Serve with shredded Fox Hill cheddar and Red Fife Crackers (page 125).

VanDine Quality Dry Beans

"We like the idea of preserving heritage," says Carolyn VanDine from her family farm near Woodstock, New Brunswick. That might be a bit of an understatement—she and her husband, Allan, have been walking their talk by producing high-quality heritage varietals for over thirty-seven years.

The VanDines grow and sell three varietals of historic prominence in the Maritimes. Terrific in salads, the Jacob's Cattle bean is the traditional baking bean in Nova Scotia. It is a large, burgundy-coloured, speckled bean with a distinctive texture and appearance. Yellow eye beans, their second varietal, have long been popular in eastern New Brunswick. The yellow eye bean is a

medium, quick-cooking bean that is especially good for soups. Finally, the soldier bean is the legume of choice in western New Brunswick, where it is most often baked with a touch of maple syrup or molasses. Both the yellow eye and the soldier have shared the spotlight in PEI.

All three beans are soft-skinned varieties, which means that instead of needing to be soaked overnight, they should be soaked for just one hour prior to cooking. VanDine Beans are widely available at stores throughout the Maritimes. For more information or to locate beans in your area, email hudini@nbnet.nb.ca or call (506) 328-3723.

Allan and Carolyn VanDine

Curry Maple Squash Bread   Yield: 1 loaf

Background flavours of almond and curry set this sweet breakfast bread apart from the everyday loaf.

Ingredients
    ½ cup butter
    1 tablespoon almond or walnut oil
    1 ½ cups all purpose flour (such as Speerville Whole White Flour)
    1 teaspoon baking soda
    ¾ teaspoon ground cinnamon
    1 teaspoon curry powder
    ½ teaspoon ground cardamom
    ½ teaspoon salt
    1 cup maple syrup
    2 large eggs
    ¾ cup Baked Squash with Walnut Oil (page 110)
    ½ cup whole milk or light cream
    1 teaspoon almond extract

Directions
    Preheat oven to 350°F and butter a loaf pan.
    In a small pan, melt butter over medium-low heat. Remove from heat and stir in almond oil. Set aside.
    Combine flour, baking soda, cinnamon, curry powder, cardamom, and salt in a mixing bowl and whisk thoroughly. In a second mixing bowl, whisk together maple syrup, eggs, baked squash, milk or cream, and almond extract. Add melted butter mixture and whisk. Add dry ingredients to wet ingredients, stir to combine, then transfer batter to buttered loaf pan. Bake for 1 hour, or until a knife inserted in the middle comes out clean.

Apple Sorbet   Serves 8

Apples have been cultivated in the Maritimes since the first Acadian orchards of the seventeenth century. Considering that those first apples were used mostly to ferment hard cider (a popular beverage among Acadians of all ages), it seems fitting to celebrate their heritage with this alcohol-infused sorbet.

Ingredients
   4 pounds apples (any variety), peeled, cored, and sliced
   2-inch piece of peeled fresh ginger
   1 bottle (750 mL) white wine (Jost Kellermeister or another sweet wine is
      a good choice)
   1 cup sugar

Directions
   Place the apples in a heavy saucepan. Crush the cut, peeled ginger with the broad side of your knife and add to the apples. Add half the wine and bring to a simmer over medium heat.

   Cook, stirring occasionally, until the apples are completely broken down, up to 2 hours (cooking time will depend on the varietal of apple used).

   Add the sugar and continue to cook, stirring, for another 5 minutes. Add the remaining wine and combine thoroughly. Transfer mixture to a freezable container and place in the freezer. Stir every 20 minutes until sorbet is frozen through, 2–3 hours.

Winter

Winter brings the longest nights of the year and then, even as the light creeps back in around the edges of the day, cold follows the dark just as heat followed the light in summer. This is the time to enjoy fall storage produce, an array of satisfying, fill-you-up foods such as beets, potatoes, cabbage, beans, winter squash, onions, carrots, parsnips, apples, and pears.

Fresh mushrooms are a common winter treat in the Maritimes. Happily, we are also experiencing a sharply increasing trend of salad greens grown locally in greenhouses throughout the winter—ask at your local farmers' market or natural foods store to discover who grows winter greens in your area.

Finally, if you were clever enough to put up produce throughout the growing season, now is the time to break out all your treats. Frozen berries and fruit syrups can put a smile on your face every morning, while dried, roasted, and sauced tomatoes can enliven your suppers throughout the winter. Don't forget canned goods, either; even if you don't have your own, many farmers offer their own excellent produce in the form of pickles, chow chow, jams, and jellies.

Berry Maple Granola   Serves 8

Don't like dried fruit in your granola? Leave it out—nothing bad will happen. The same goes for the nuts. You can even adjust the sweeteners up or down to suit your tastes. No matter how you like your granola, though, once you taste this full-bodied recipe no supermarket substitute will do.

Ingredients
- 4 cups rolled oats (such as Speerville New Found Oatmeal)
- 1 stick (½ cup) butter, melted
- 1 cup chopped nuts and/or seeds (walnuts, almonds, cashews, sunflower seeds, poppy seeds, etc.)
- ½ cup maple syrup, local honey, or a combination
- 1 teaspoon vanilla extract
- 1 ½ cups dried chopped fruit (cranberries, blueberries, and apples are some of my Maritime faves)
- ¼ cup minced candied ginger (optional)

Directions

Preheat the oven to 300°F.

Thoroughly combine rolled oats and melted butter in a mixing bowl. Transfer to a rimmed cookie sheet or large baking dish and spread out evenly.

Bake for 45–55 minutes, stirring every 10 minutes, until oats are lightly coloured. Add chopped nuts and/or seeds 20 minutes into the baking time and stir in thoroughly.

In a second bowl, combine maple syrup or honey with vanilla extract. Pour syrup mixture over oats, stir thoroughly, and bake for 5 more minutes. Remove granola from the oven and allow to cool.

Add dried fruit and candied ginger if using, stir thoroughly, and serve or store in a covered container. Will keep, refrigerated, for up to 2 weeks.

Charlie's Carrot Soup   Serves 6

When my son was four, we read Carrot Soup *by John Segal—after which he insisted on making carrot soup, of course. (I'm embarrassed to tell you how many of my dishes are developed at the insistence of a young child.) This was a simple recipe we devised after a bit of trial and error, and it's still a staple in our home.*

Ingredients

   2 tablespoons butter
   1 large onion, minced
   1 cup chopped green carrot tops, cleaned and firmly packed (optional)
   2 teaspoons salt
   3 pounds carrots, peeled and thinly sliced
   6 cups Chicken Stock (page 102) or Vegetable Stock (page 59)
   2 tablespoons minced fresh dill
   Pepper to taste

Directions

   Heat a pot on medium-low heat. Add butter, onion, carrot tops, and salt. Cook, stirring occasionally, for 20 minutes.

   Add carrots and chicken stock. Increase heat to high and bring to a boil, then reduce heat to medium, cover, and simmer for 30 minutes.

   Purée mixture with an immersion blender or remove to a stand blender, purée, then return to a clean pot.

   Sprinkle with dill and pepper. Serve hot.

Note the carrot tops: If you buy carrots with the tops on, don't chuck them in the trash or the compost. Also delicious in salads, they add a great depth of flavour and nutrition for your own little bunny.

Red Fife Crackers   Yield: approximately 4 dozen crackers

I was delighted to learn that Speerville Flour Mill produces Red Fife flour. A hard wheat with a particularly high protein content, Red Fife is part and parcel of Canada's history. At one time the most popular wheat in the country, it nearly died out twice—once by hungry cows, once by human neglect—but has made an impressive comeback as part of contemporary, flavourful Canadian cuisine.

Ingredients
> 3 cups Red Fife flour, plus extra for flouring the counter
> 2 teaspoons salt
> ½ teaspoon dried minced rosemary
> 1 cup plain, full fat yogurt (available from Fox Hill Cheese House)
> ½ cup room-temperature butter

Directions
> Preheat oven to 450°F.
> Combine all ingredients in a mixing bowl. Wash your hands very well with soap and water, then knead the dough by hand until it forms a smooth ball.
> Sprinkle flour on a clean counter and on your rolling pin. Separate the ball of dough into 4 equal parts. Roll out each quarter very thin, cutting crackers of your desired shape and size with a cookie cutter, pizza cutter, or sharp knife. Transfer the cut crackers to an ungreased baking sheet.
> If desired, brush each cracker with melted butter. Bake until browned, 7–9 minutes. Transfer to a rack to cool. Enjoy plain or with any desired topping. These are delicious with Picante Tomato Dip (page 127).

Picante Tomato Dip   Serves 8

This dip is often featured at the weekly "Friday afternoon office party" in our home. Enjoy it with friends, family, and fresh fruit!

Ingredients
    ¼ cup Oven-Dried Tomatoes (page 70), minced
    8 ounces cream cheese or Fox Hill quark
    1 cup plain yogurt (available from Fox Hill Cheese House)
    1 teaspoon Garlic Chile Sauce (page 60) or other hot sauce
    Salt and pepper to taste

Directions
    Thoroughly blend all the ingredients and serve with Red Fife Crackers (page 125), chips, toast, or raw vegetables.

Carrot Cumin Purée   Serves 4

Did you know that carrots weren't always orange? In fact, the orange carrot was developed in the sixteenth century as a horticultural tribute to William of Orange— prior to that, most carrots were either white or purple! Today you can find white, yellow, and purple carrots at many farmers' markets and natural foods stores. Try a blend of coloured carrots in this recipe for a rich taste and wide nutritional profile.

Ingredients
- 1 pound carrots, peeled and sliced into rounds
- 2 garlic cloves, peeled and minced or pressed
- 2 teaspoons ground cumin
- 1 cup Chicken Stock (page 102) or Vegetable Stock (page 59)
- ¼ cup heavy cream
- 1 tablespoon butter

Directions

Combine carrots, garlic, cumin, and stock in a saucepan. Simmer over medium heat until carrots are very tender, about 15 minutes. Remove from heat, add cream and butter, and purée with an immersion blender or remove to a stand blender. Serve immediately.

Note: Purée carrots before adding the cream and butter for a compact, highly versatile base that freezes wonderfully. You can heat and add cream and butter to complete the purée, add an extra cup of stock to make a soup, replace the cumin with your favourite herbs or seasonings, or leave the garlic, cumin, butter, and cream out to make baby food.

Roasted Tomato and Lentils   Serves 4

This dish makes a great pick-me-up lunch in the middle of a busy workday. Leave out the spices if you'd rather—between the stock, onion, and tomatoes, you won't want for flavour.

Ingredients
- ¼ cup extra-virgin olive oil
- 1 large onion, minced
- 1 ½ tablespoons curry powder
- 2 teaspoons ground ginger
- 4 cups Chicken Stock (page 102) or Vegetable Stock (page 59)
- 2 cups red lentils, rinsed (available from Speerville)
- 3 cups Slow-Roasted Tomatoes (page 64)
- Salt and pepper to taste
- ½ cup plain yogurt (available from Fox Hill Cheese House)

Directions

Heat olive oil in a stock pot over medium-high heat. Add minced onion and sauté for 5 minutes. Add curry powder and ground ginger and sauté for 1 additional minute, stirring constantly.

Add stock and lentils and bring to boil. Reduce heat to low, cover, and simmer until lentils are fully cooked and starting to dissolve, about 45 minutes.

Add tomatoes and season to taste with salt and pepper. Stir to blend. Serve with a dollop of yogurt on each serving.

Happy Jack Pork   Serves 4

Serve this deceptively simple tenderloin with mashed potatoes and Carrot Cumin Purée (page 129) to warm your loved ones from tip to toe.

Ingredients
   2 pounds pork tenderloin

Marinade
   ½ cup apple brandy (available from Ironworks Distillery)
   ½ cup maple syrup
   ½ cup Garlic Chile Sauce (page 60) or Sriracha

Sauce
   ½ cup apple brandy
   ⅓ cup garlic chile sauce or Sriracha
   ¼ cup maple syrup
   ½ cup heavy cream (substitute light cream, whole milk, or even rice milk if you wish)

Directions
   Thoroughly mix all ingredients for the marinade, then submerge the tenderloin in the marinade and refrigerate, covered, for 8–12 hours.
   Preheat oven to 375°F. Place pork with marinade in a baking pan and bake for 45–60 minutes (depending on the size and shape of your tenderloin) until internal temperature is 150°F.
   Remove pork from oven and set aside to rest for 10 minutes. Meanwhile, prepare sauce by thoroughly combining the apple brandy, maple syrup, and garlic chile sauce in a saucepan and bring to a boil over medium-high heat. Boil for 5 minutes, remove from heat, and whisk in cream. Plate the pork and drizzle with sauce. Serve with a side of Autumn Fruit Sauce (page 88) if desired.

Ironworks Distillery

The local fruit-focused Ironworks Distillery in Lunenburg, Nova Scotia, is one of the first micro-distilleries in the Maritimes. Pierre Guevremont and Lynne MacKay opened the business in their heritage blacksmith's shop in 2009 and have been continually expanding their product line since. Not only do their spirits and liqueurs compliment many recipes, but they are created with a panorama of Nova Scotia fruits.

For starters, Pierre and Lynne use Annapolis Valley apples for their unique apple-based vodka and apple brandy. They've experimented with different varietals, including Macintosh, Jonagold, Golden Delicious, and Cortland; their favourite is Russet, although there's also a 100 percent Honeycrisp batch of brandy in the works.

Cranberries come from Terra Beata Cranberry Farms on Heckman Island, Lunenburg County, and wild blueberries from Van Dyk Farms in Queen's County. Their pears are grown at Boates Orchards (page 38). Continuing the trend of sourcing as locally as possible, they even use molasses imported by Crosby Molasses Company of Saint John, New Brunswick, for their rum. For more information and a full product list, visit their website at ironworksdistillery.com or call (902) 640-2424.

Ironworks Distillery at sunset in Lunenburg, Nova Scotia

Pierre Guevremont and Lynne MacKay, proprietors of Ironworks Distillery

Spicy Cod Brandade   Serves 4

*It would just be wrong to leave salt cod out of a Maritime cookbook, so here you go—
an updated take on a seaside classic.*

Ingredients
   ⅓ pound skinless boneless salt cod
   2 large potatoes
   1 cup Crème Fraîche (page 15)
   3 cloves garlic, peeled and crushed
   1 minced dried hot pepper (jalapeño, habanero, Scotch bonnet, or similar)
   ¼ cup Herbed Mayonnaise (page 40)
   Pepper to taste
   Loaf of crusty bread, sliced and toasted

Directions
   Rinse cod well to remove external salt. Place in a bowl and cover with 2 inches
of cold water. Soak in the refrigerator for 24 hours, changing water 3 times.
   Peel potatoes and cut into 1-inch pieces. Put in a saucepan and cover with 1
inch of well-salted water. Bring to a boil and simmer potatoes until very tender,
about 15 minutes. (Do not drain until ready to whip.)
   While potatoes are cooking, bring crème fraîche to a simmer with garlic and
hot pepper in a small saucepan, then simmer gently, partially covered, until
garlic is tender, about 15 minutes.
   Meanwhile, drain cod and transfer to another large saucepan with enough
water to cover. Bring just to a simmer over medium heat, then immediately
remove from heat. (Cod should just flake; do not boil or it will become tough.)
   Drain cod and potatoes in a colander and, while still warm, combine in a large
bowl with crème fraîche mixture. Beat with an electric mixer at low speed until
combined well. Continue to beat, adding herbed mayonnaise and pepper. Top
toasted bread slices with warm brandade just before serving.

Potato Gratin   Serves 4

This recipe will blow any diet out of the water—but frankly, it's worth it. Enjoy!

Ingredients

    3 large potatoes, scrubbed clean, peeled, and cut in thin slices

    ¾ cup Havarti, sliced or shredded (available from Fox Hill Cheese House, their dill and chive or Italian herbs and spices both work particularly well)

    ¾ cup Crème Fraîche (page 15)

    Salt and pepper to taste

Directions

Preheat the oven to 350°F and butter a 9-by-12-inch baking dish.

Arrange a layer of potato slices on the bottom, then cover them with a layer of Havarti. Alternate layers of potato and cheese, finishing with a layer of cheese on top. Gently drizzle crème fraîche over the cheese and potatoes, then season the top layer with salt and pepper.

Bake for 1 hour or until potatoes are browned on top and tender when stuck with a fork.

Oyster Dressing   Serves 8

It's best to make this dressing separately from the turkey, especially if you're using the slow-roasting method described on page 140.

Ingredients

8 cups stale breadcrumbs (I use a sourdough loaf I get at my farmers' market, but any good bread will do)

2 tablespoons extra-virgin olive oil

1 large onion, finely chopped

1 cup shredded carrot

2 teaspoons dried summer savory

2 teaspoons dried thyme

3 cloves garlic, peeled and minced or pressed

½ cup melted butter

¾ cup shredded ham

12 oysters, shucked, drained, and chopped

2 cups Chicken Stock (page 102)

½ teaspoon salt

¼ teaspoon pepper

Directions

Preheat oven to 350°F. Butter a 9-by-12-inch baking dish.

Place bread crumbs in a large baking pan or a rimmed baking sheet. Toast until golden, about 30 minutes, stirring once. Set aside to cool.

Combine olive oil, onion, carrot, summer savory, thyme, and garlic in a pan. Cook over medium heat, stirring occasionally, for 15 minutes.

In a large mixing bowl, combine toasted bread crumbs, vegetable mixture, melted butter, ham, oysters, stock, salt, and pepper. Toss well.

Transfer dressing to the baking dish and bake for 60 minutes. Cool for 10 minutes, then serve.

Aspy Bay Oysters

Alex Dunphy has lived in South Harbour, at the northern tip of Cape Breton, his entire life. Along with his wife, Susan, and their four sons, he has been involved in the oyster business since 1985. They gave the name "Aspy Bay Oyster" to the local oysters and have been sharing them with fortunate visitors ever since.

The deep, cold waters of South Harbour are ideal for oyster life. The Dunphys own a federally licensed processing plant with two upwellers to increase the nutrient flow and growth rate of juvenile oysters. Alex selects and gathers oysters by hand; Susan sorts and grades them. The resulting oysters are

sublime—salty with a delicate texture and a crisp, sweet finish.

Aspy Bay is one of many excellent local oyster purveyors along the coastline in the Maritimes. When purchasing oysters for preparation at home, keep them moist in ice and refrigerated below 5°C. Purchase Aspy Bay oysters at the Hideaway Campground & Oyster Market in South Harbour or enjoy them at one of several restaurants along the Cabot Trail. For more information, email info@campingcapebreton.com or call (902) 383-2116.

Slow-Roasted Heritage Turkey in Juniper Brine   Serves 8–10

Even if you can't eat local every day, going the extra mile to cook a locally raised, free-range turkey for the holidays is a special way to feed your family with love. You can also use this method to roast a chicken or any other poultry you wish.

Ingredients

    10 cups water
    2 cups salt
    1 cup local honey
    1 local free-range turkey, 12–16 pounds (a heritage variety if you can get it—ask at your local farmers' market)
    8 large garlic cloves, peeled
    ¼ cup dried juniper berries
    3 bay leaves
    2 tablespoons pepper
    4–6 sprigs fresh herbs (thyme, rosemary, sage, or a mixture)
    2 tablespoons extra-virgin olive oil
    4 cups Chicken Stock (page 102)

Directions

In a large pan, combine water, salt, and honey. Warm over medium heat, stirring occasionally, until salt and honey dissolve. Add garlic, juniper berries, bay leaves, and pepper. Stir to combine, then remove brine mixture from heat.

Rinse turkey thoroughly, then place inside a large stock pot or a large food bag. Carefully pour the brine into the pot or bag with the turkey. If using a bag, press out excess air so that turkey is completely enveloped in brine, then tie shut. Store in the refrigerator for at least 12 and as many as 24 hours.

Begin cooking the night before you'll be serving the turkey. Preheat oven to 415°F, remove turkey from the brine, and place in a roasting pan. Place herb sprigs in the body cavity. Rub the skin with olive oil. Pour chicken stock in the bottom of the roasting pan. Cook the turkey until browned on top, 30–40 minutes, then lower the temperature to 200°F.

Roast overnight. Most turkeys will cook in 40–50 minutes a pound at this temperature, but birds can vary widely, so gauge doneness by temperature, not time. In the morning, check the internal temperature by plunging a meat thermometer into the thickest part of the meat. Check occasionally throughout the day until meat reaches a temperature of 185°F, then remove from oven. If it's done too early in the day, turn the temperature of the oven down to 185 °F and keep the turkey in the oven until 1 hour before eating. If it doesn't seem like it will be done on time, turn the temperature up to 225 °F to finish roasting. Allow to rest for 30 minutes after removing from oven, then carve and serve.

Note: Many newer ovens turn themselves off after 12 hours (trust me; I learned the hard way!) so check yours. Don't worry if the meat has a pinkish tone; as long as it reaches 185°F, it's safe to eat.

Celebration Fruit Cake   Yield: 1 loaf

I like fruit, I like nuts, I like booze, I like cake...so why don't I like fruitcake? Probably because most recipes prioritize durability over delectability, with fruits that are chosen for colour, rather than taste. This recipe gives you a guaranteed result that is both delicious and traditional.

Ingredients
- ½ cup dried blueberries
- ½ cup dried raspberries
- ½ cup dried apples, chopped
- ½ cup dried pears, chopped
- ½ cup dried peaches, chopped
- ¾ cup pear eau de vie (available from Ironworks Distillery) or other favourite fruit-based liqueur
- ½ cup local honey
- 1 ¾ cups all purpose flour (such as Speerville Whole White Flour)
- 2 teaspoons baking powder
- ¼ teaspoon salt
- ½ teaspoon ground nutmeg
- ¼ teaspoon ground cloves
- 1 teaspoon ground cinnamon
- ½ cup plain whole-milk yogurt (available from Fox Hill Cheese House)
- 2 tablespoons sunflower oil
- ¾ cup (1 ½ sticks) butter, room temperature
- 3 large eggs
- 1 ½ cups crushed hazelnuts (or other sliced or crushed nuts as desired)

Directions

Position rack in centre of oven and preheat to 350°F. Butter 2 loaf pans.

Combine blueberries, raspberries, apples, pears, peaches, eau de vie, and honey in a mixing bowl and set aside.

In a second mixing bowl, combine flour, baking powder, salt, nutmeg, cloves, and cinnamon. Whisk thoroughly.

In a third mixing bowl, beat together yogurt, oil, butter, and eggs. Add dry ingredients and beat until well blended. Gently fold in fruit mixture and hazelnuts. Divide batter between the buttered loaf pans.

Bake until a knife inserted into the centre of each loaf comes out clean, about 50 minutes. Cool in pans for 30 minutes, then turn out onto racks. This cake keeps in the refrigerator for 1 week or in the freezer for 2 months, so feel free to make this new holiday favourite ahead of time.

Pistachio Halibut   Serves 4

Halibut is a hearty fish—this simple yet luxuriously rich preparation accentuates the beefsteak-like quality of the flesh.

Ingredients

  1 pound boneless skinless halibut fillets or cheeks
  ¾ cup heavy cream
  ⅓ cup natural (undyed) pistachios, finely chopped
  3 tablespoons cornmeal (available from Speerville)
  ¾ teaspoon salt
  ½ teaspoon black pepper
  ¼ cup extra-virgin olive oil

Directions

Place halibut in a baking dish, pour cream over fish, cover, and chill for 30 minutes, turning over once.

Stir pistachios, cornmeal, salt, and pepper together in a bowl.

Remove fish from cream, shaking off any excess. Dredge in the cornmeal-pistachio mixture. Place the coated fish on a clean plate.

Heat olive oil in a frying pan over medium-high heat, then sauté fish, turning over once, until golden and just cooked through, 3–4 minutes per side. Remove to a serving plate and serve immediately.

Merry Christmas Custard   Serves 6

Leave some of this smooth, spicy concoction out for Santa. As much as he loves cookies, by the time he gets to Canada he's dying for something made with an actual vegetable!

Ingredients

  3 cups half and half cream (18 percent milkfat)
  6 large eggs
  ¾ cup local honey
  ⅓ cup molasses
  2 teaspoons cinnamon
  2 teaspoons ginger
  1 teaspoon nutmeg
  ¼ teaspoon ground cloves
  ¼ teaspoon salt
  3 cups Baked Squash with Walnut Oil (page 110) or canned pumpkin purée
  Whipped cream to taste
  ½ cup gingersnap crumbs

Directions

   Preheat oven to 325°F and butter a medium baking dish. Put 2 inches of water into a larger baking dish and set the buttered dish inside it.

   Heat the 18 percent cream in a heavy saucepan over medium heat just to the boiling point, then immediately remove from heat.

   Beat the eggs, honey, molasses, cinnamon, ginger, nutmeg, cloves, and salt together until thoroughly blended. Add the heated 18 percent cream and the baked squash and mix until smooth. Pour the mixture into the buttered baking dish.

   Bake for 50 minutes or until a knife plunged into the middle comes out clean. Cool to room temperature, then refrigerate overnight. Top with whipped cream and gingersnap crumbs just before serving.

Index

Photo credits

All photos by Nancy McCarthy, with the following exceptions:

Page 19: Courtesy of Speerville Flour Mill
Page 21, 29, 38, 54, 61, 139, 146: Courtesy of Elisabeth Bailey
Page 53: Courtesy of Ron and Joanne Schmidt
Page 69: Courtesy of Gus and Sandra Hargrove
Page 76: Courtesy of Fox Hill Cheese House
Page 114: Courtesy of Allan and Carolyn VanDine
Page 132, 133: Courtesy of Ironworks Distillery

Other cookbooks from Nimbus Publishing

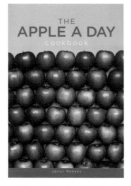

The Apple A Day
Cookbook

Atlantic Seafood

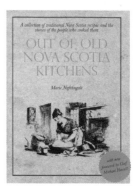

Out of Old
Nova Scotia
Kitchens

Favourite Recipes
from Old
New Brunswick
Kitchens

The Taste of
Nova Scotia
Cookbook